Using Stories to Make Art:
Creative Activities Using Children's Literature

D1561190

$\mathcal{U}$sing Stories to Make Art:

Creative Activities Using Children's Literature

Wendy M. L. Libby

THOMSON

DELMAR LEARNING

Australia Canada Mexico Singapore Spain United Kingdom United States

THOMSON
™
DELMAR LEARNING

Using Stories to Make Art: Creative Activities Using Children's Literature
Wendy M. L. Libby

Vice President, Career Ed SBU:
Dawn Gerrain

Acquisitions Editor:
Erin O'Connor

Developmental Editor:
Alexis Ferraro

Editorial Assistant:
Ivy Ip

Director of Production:
Wendy A. Troeger

Production Coordinator:
Nina Tucciarelli

Director of Marketing:
Donna J. Lewis

Channel Manager:
Stephen Smith

Composition:
Larry O'Brien

Library of Congress Cataloging-in-Publication Data

Libby, Wendy M. L.
    Using stories to make art : creative activities using children's literature / by Wendy M.L. Libby.
        p. cm.
    Includes bibliographical references.
    ISBN 1-4018-3467-1
    1. Art—Study and teaching (Elementary)— Activity programs.
    2. Children's literature—Study and teaching (Elementary) I. Title.
    N350.L43 2003
    372.5'044—dc21   2003043839

To my family who upholds the message of believing in yourself
and to my Aunt Annette whose artistic creativity is an inspiration.

$\mathcal{C}$ontents

Contents

Preface

Art experiences are of value to all children. They allow for self-expression, self-realization, and a connection to the world around them. Repeated exposure to art sharpens the perception of children.

Visual arts education should be an essential part of every school curriculum. It should be a sequential program with emphasis on activity and process. Children should be given the opportunity to observe, discriminate, interpret, make decisions, solve problems, compare, and explore through discovery. An art program allows for creative expression. We all have a need to express ourselves, and art can stimulate communication. Art is the center of human experience connecting dream with reality. It is a balance of a child's intellect and his or her emotions.

Art involves independent thinking, exploration, problem solving, creativity, and expression with freedom that encourages self-confidence. Art is an activity, a way of seeing the world and relating to it. Children understand best what they experience personally, and art is an experience. Art experiences are first perceived through our senses, and therefore we need to assist our children to develop upon the things they see, hear, and feel in their environment. In an art class, a child is not merely being taught the skills of drawing, painting, printing, sculpting, cutting and pasting, but is being guided to see what is in his/her environment, to respond to it, and to visually express it.

During the 25 years that I have been an elementary art teacher, I have found that my favorite place to experience inspiration is the library. I am always able to find information on the subject areas that the classrooms are learning about in order to plan art lessons. This reinforces the students' knowledge of these subjects through visual creativity. Books can encourage the ability to look at the world differently. They encourage critical thinking about learning and situations in life. Picture books can be a motivating source of ideas. Book illustrations can work in combination with the text or independently to reinforce concepts of learning. Illustrations expose children to varieties in art. They might reflect the artistic style of when the story takes place or the cultural style of where it takes place. The variety of artistic style and media expose children to a variety of artistic techniques.

Creativity lies within everyone to some degree, yet it is hard to determine the source from where it comes. It is often shaped by a person's abilities, the opportunities open to him or her, and the demands at the time of the endeavor. Creativeness can be nurtured by seeking new ways to express individuality. Creative people are curious, independent in thought, and open to new experiences. They are flexible and are always seeking new solutions. Creative people tend to have better self-awareness and self-acceptance. It is important that they trust their own judgment. Art activities offer opportunities for establishing conditions that promote the development of creativity. It is necessary for children to understand that there is not just one right answer in art. Allowing children to work freely with spontaneity encourages creativity.

The lessons in this book are a series of interactive literary-based art activities that encourage exploration into specific educational concepts. They are based around art elements and principles. Opportunity is given for students to work with a variety of materials and techniques. The primary goal is to focus on the process of creating. The activities provided are certainly not the only ways to approach learning the stated concepts. There are many ways to extend the ideas presented in this book. Activities can be altered to meet specific classroom needs. Students truly enjoy creating their own work and the benefits of the arts are priceless.

Acknowledgments

The author acknowledges:

- the authors and illustrators who spark creative imagination in us all.

- the librarians who find just the right book for just the right reason.

- the children, teachers, and colleagues whose creative discoveries are endless.

- the following reviewers for their noteworthy opinions:

Billie Armstrong
Tyrrell County Head Start
Columbia, NC

Jody Martin
Children's World Learning Centers
Golden, CO

Patricia Capistron
Rocking Unicorn Preschool
West Chatham, MA

Sandy Wlaschin
University of Nebraska–Omaha
Omaha, NE

Victoria Folds, Ed.D.
Tutor Time Learning Systems
Boca Raton, FL

- the publisher and editors who helped make this book possible.

About This Book

Art is vital to learning experiences. It improves student performance in other subject areas. By working with the visual characteristics of design elements (line, shape, color, value, texture, form, and space) and the design principles (balance, emphasis, movement, repetition, rhythm, unity, and variety), areas of classroom study can be reflected upon to advantage.

Though the lessons in this book guide students to observe and create works based on the stories and illustrations, it is necessary to allow the freedom of self-expression. Oftentimes talking with children about their ideas helps to get them started on their own creative thought process. Even though children use the same subject for their work, their individual interpretations still differ. The same materials and elements might be used, but the compositional arrangements and the choice of details will be different and individual variations will be noted. The activities in this book are directed, which means that an adult initiates the activity, the materials are supplied, and the topic is proposed. The lessons can be approached as given, or they can merely be stepping-stones to other creative activities. Alternate materials can be supplied, which might change the technique. Motivational themes can be altered allowing for a different subject focus, and different books could be used to introduce the activity. The activities are suggestions to assist the teacher yet by no means are meant to be rigid. The book gives activities in a step-by-step fashion, but the teacher, supervisor, or caregiver should be able to alter the steps or directions according to the abilities and skills of the children. It is necessary to assume that creations will vary and will promote individuality. The activities will focus on the elements and principles of art and will provide a background of information for children to refer to when making their own spontaneous drawings. Children gain insight by being exposed to a variety of stimulus pictures of subjects they can relate to. Their surroundings interest them, and these often receive careful attention in their own work.

Art plays an important role in the curriculum, and this book promotes the integration of art and children's literature. Each art lesson is combined with a children's book. These books are easily found in children's own collections, at schools, or in local libraries. It is not necessary to find the exact book in order to introduce the lesson. Books with similar subject matters or books with similar illustration techniques would also allow a successful activity. Other reference materials and teaching tools can be gathered on the various subjects proposed in the stories and can be connected to other areas of the curriculum. The lessons in the book emphasize a connection between visual and verbal expression. Learning results from stimuli, and children learn better when a learning experience is reinforced by other learning experiences. Children find learning easier through sensory means, and visual and verbal expression encourages successful learning in a satisfying way. The art activities in this book offer experimentation with a variety of materials. The resulting creative expression can be integrated with all classroom curricula.

The activities in this book guide children to a disciplined and discriminating approach to their art. Being exposed to art vocabulary will make it easier to find expression. The wide range of stimuli, materials, and techniques presented will permit greater overall flexibility in a child's expressiveness. Attention must be given to detail, and a teacher can guide children to experience their environment through their senses. Looking closely at details and finding ways to direct attention to sensory experiences are all part of the teacher's role. A demonstration should include audiovisuals along with the handling of materials. The demonstration often stimulates the children and motivates them to begin their own artwork. After the presentation of the lesson, time must be given for children to experiment with new techniques and ideas and explore possibilities.

All art activities presented here are based on a well-thought-out sequence. The activities are detailed plans for a step-by-step lesson. Although the lessons are presented in certain steps, exploration and imagination are encouraged. Emphasis should be on the process. The lessons include the concept/objectives, which are the purpose of the lesson. All needed materials are listed for the lesson given; however, materials can be added, deleted, or changed for more open ended projects.

Depending on the amount of time allowed for the activity, either the children's books can be read or a summary can be given while the students look at the illustrations. As the story is read or retold, students are encouraged to pay attention to details. Information about the illustrations should be pointed out and discussed. The lessons are based on a one-hour class period, yet again a teacher, supervisor, or caregiver can alter the time based on individual situations. During the activities/process part of the lesson, while looking at the illustrations, the concepts of the lesson can be brought into mind. For example, lines, shapes, or textures might be noted, or how the illustrator showed movement. The presentation of the art project requires a demonstration of the use of materials. The steps in the process are sequentially listed. Each lesson has a few questions for discussion to help focus on the concepts of the lesson and reinforce the learning that is taking place.

The purpose for discussion questions is to focus on the objectives of the lesson. This is an opportunity for teachers to allow students to connect visual expression with verbal expression. In order to have children think more critically, it is necessary to use questioning strategies that allow children to answer beyond the simple description and recall. The way questions are asked can engage students in reasoning, speculating, and discriminating. It is necessary to guide students in a meaningful discussion that develops understanding and appreciation of art. Curriculum learning can be strengthened and enhanced at this time. Share time should be allowed so that children can view and discuss each other's work. Their ideas and feelings should be expressed in order for them to truly appreciate the varieties of other students' creativity. Discussion and evaluation helps students develop a higher level of thinking. Students need to use multiple thinking operations to solve problems. They use basic thinking operations that relate to all learning areas. It allows for recall of information, achievement of goals during the creation of the artwork, and aesthetic perception and valuing. Students should see themselves as artists, and this can be facilitated when their work and the work of their peers are shown as forms of art.

Activity Level Guide

Easy

Medium

Advanced

The activity guide level is a quick notation of the developmental level of the lesson. An icon listing of easy, medium, and advanced is shown with each lesson to help rate the activity by the experience needed. All children do not reach the same skill level at the same time. They grow and develop at different rates, and it is important to allow for individual skills and creative abilities. The lessons termed easy allow the students to receive a solid base, and as the lessons move to moderate and advanced, the students will experience new levels of complexity. Some experiences that are labeled easy may even seem difficult to some children, and some that are labeled advanced could be achieved and enjoyed by younger children. It is necessary to guide the students in such a way that they will be able to express themselves within the guidelines of the lesson and have a personal meaningful experience. The lessons are suggestions and can be modified according to needs of the children who are participating. A sample idea is illustrated. However, creations will vary, and it is important to allow for individual skills and creative abilities where experimentation, exploration, process, and expression of oneself are more important.

Curriculum extensions are ideas where teachers, supervisors, or caregivers can connect the art activity with other dimensions of the curriculum. The ideas listed are for varying age levels and skill abilities, so it would be necessary to alter the suggestions accordingly. For example, preschool children would not be able to research different kinds of bears, but a teacher could show them pictures of different kinds of bears and they could talk about how the colors or the sizes of the bears might be different. Preschool children would not be able to write a poem themselves, but they could create a poem together with the teacher. Older children would not do some of the finger play songs that the preschoolers would enjoy, but for variety purposes and to spark an idea for someone reading the book, different levels are listed under the same activity.

This book will aid in simplifying instruction and reducing the amount of preparation needed by clearly stating what each lesson involves. Not only will it be extremely helpful to a new teacher, but it will also assist experienced teachers who are looking for novel approaches to integrate art with other subjects.

$\mathcal{I}$ntroduction

Art is unique to each child, and as each child experiences the freedom of production through an art process, there is a connection with the world. Children learn best through observation and experience. Through observation children develop a sensitive and sensational record. Children are introduced to visual images from their earliest consciousness.

A connection with illustrations and stories is made at a very young age. Books become an integral part of a child's life from infancy on. Authors and illustrators make connections with their young audiences as children are read to and taught how to read. This process helps them to grow as individuals. Children's books stimulate children to the world around them, and they can relate to it by responding through art.

They acquire enthusiasm and excitement about their world through stories and illustrations, and they are able to reply creatively through art experiences. Art activities inspire young readers. When children make their own artwork based on illustrations from children's books, not only do they have an outlet for creativity, but they also gain a meaningful way to experience language arts. Stories selected should entice listeners to become involved and want to relate their own version. Children gain an insight into the literary process by celebrating books through illustrations. A connection to books is made, and children's knowledge of the scope of literature is enlarged. Children become captivated with what is, was, and might be in fiction and nonfiction books. When children are urged to illustrate and tell stories, they are gaining insight into the literary process. They are able to practice creativity and discover a meaningful way to use the language arts. This process combines two means of self-expression: art and language.

As children look through the illustrations in books, they are introduced to the subject and content of the story. Whether counting books, alphabet books, books on animals, space, or transportation, fact or fiction, children share vivid visual connections. They can relate spontaneously to the story with their own artwork as well as embellish the story with their own ideas. Books can trigger questions, thoughts, and the desire for more knowledge. Children gain knowledge when they are surrounded with subjects that capture their interest. They can be attracted to these subjects through art experiences. Stories can be shared, and connections can be made to any area of the curriculum. Storytelling, like art, is basic to all cultures, and both areas can enrich all other areas of the curriculum. They both provide incentive for further research and require planning, developing, and organizing thoughts. Retelling a story is a way to provide opportunities for students to participate in the story. Extended participation can be achieved through individual response given in a related art project.

Art is a means of self-development and self-expression. Exploration can stem from the visual connection. By allowing children the freedom to express themselves through art experiences, their attitudes toward learning will flourish. The way children create artwork depends on their ability to interpret their observations, their skill development, their insight into the materials being used, and the extent to which they can give form to their inner visions. The use of books and illustrations as motivational experiences will extend learning, and the integration of curricular subjects can occur with related topics. Exposure to a variety of illustrations of various subject matters strengthens interest, and children become more aware and more responsive to their surroundings and their world. Art projects can be stepping-stones to other activities and integrated into all areas of classroom teaching.

Whether teaching math, science, social studies, or other curricular subjects, children's interests will be intrigued through illustrations in books, and their observation, knowledge, and reflection will be strengthened by their involvement in a related art experience.

When children create, they include the things that they know about and that are important to them. They need to establish some kind of relationship. This relationship combines the children's knowledge of things and their own personal connections. Connections are fostered by experiences that we have with things. Children should enjoy discovering and exploring the world around them and acquire the ability to think independently and creatively, all of which can be developed through art activities.

Although this book focuses on art and children's literature, art should not be taught only through children's literature. The use of literature is yet another approach that teachers can use in providing their students with varied art experiences. Illustrations, as well as the subject being introduced, motivate children. The trend in education is going toward the use of an integrated curriculum by presenting material in an interrelated context. Using literature and illustrations to introduce curriculum provides situations to make learning more personal.

Activities

Alphabetically Listed

Alligator

Objectives/Concepts

1. To work with shape and color.
2. To experiment with cutting and pasting technique.
3. To create pattern.
4. To create texture.

Technique

Cutting and Pasting

Materials

6 in. x 18 in. green paper
6 in. x 9 in. green paper (2 per student)
2 in. x 3 in. green paper (4 per student)
4½ in. x 6 in. yellow paper
4½ in. x 6 in. black paper (2 per student)
White paper scraps
Scissors
Glue
Black crayon

Alternate Materials

Markers, tempera paint, paper varieties

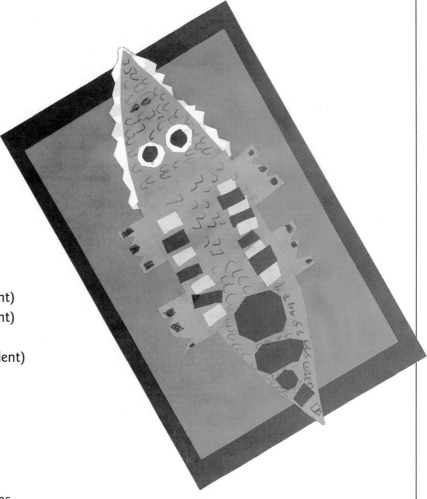

Activities/Process

1. Read or give a summary of the book *Keep Your Mouth Closed, Dear* by Aliki, focusing on the illustrations.
2. Cut a triangle from each 6 in. x 9 in. green paper by cutting from the center point of a 6 in. side diagonally to the corners of the other 6 in. side.
3. Glue one of these triangles to each side of the long green paper so that the 6 in. sides match, making the head and tail.
4. Cut little triangles from one of 2 in. edges of the four small green papers and glue the straight side to the large rectangle to make the four legs.
5. Cut strips from the yellow and one piece of black paper about ½ to 1 inch wide.

6. Cut strips into squares or rectangles.
7. Arrange the squares or rectangles into patterns on the back of the alligator and glue down.
8. With the other black paper, cut squares in varying sizes.
9. Round the corners of the squares to make varying sized circles.
10. Glue the circles onto the tail from the largest size to the smallest size.
11. With black crayon, draw some U- or V-shaped lines on the face for texture.
12. With white scraps, cut triangles for the teeth and circles for the eyes. Smaller black circles can be layered onto the white.

Questions for Discussion

What shapes did you use to make the alligator? How did you make a triangle shape from a rectangle? How did you make a circle from a square? How did you show texture? What did you do to make two or more of the same shape in the same size?

Share Time/Evaluation

_____

_____

_____

_____

Curriculum Connection

Science, Social Studies, Math, Language Arts, Music, Physical Education

Curriculum Extensions

Science: Compare and contrast a crocodile and an alligator.

Social Studies: Look up where alligators and crocodiles live and locate on a map.

Math: Make different shapes in different sizes and arrange them from largest to smallest. Make different patterns using squares and rectangles in different colors.

Language Arts: Read other books about alligators. Make up your own story about an alligator. Write a poem about an alligator. Write a paragraph about what could happen if you do not keep your mouth closed.

Music: Sing songs about alligators.

Physical Education: Move around like an alligator.

Owl Babies

Baby Owls

Objectives/Concepts

1. To work with shape and color.
2. To experiment with printing.
3. To experiment with cutting and pasting technique.
4. To create texture.
5. To explore paper tearing.

Technique

Printing, Cutting and Pasting

Materials

12 in. x 18 in. blue paper
6 in. x 12 in. brown paper
Colored paper scraps (green, yellow, black)
Tempera paint (white, brown, yellow)
Sponges in 1 in. pieces
Scissors
Glue

Alternate Materials

Chalk, tissue paper

Activities/Process

1. Read or give a summary of the book *Owl Babies* by Martin Waddell, focusing on the illustrations.
2. Using a sponge and white paint, create two or three oval shapes side by side.
3. With brown paint, gently press the sponge a few times over the white.
4. With yellow paint, gently press the sponge a few times over the white and brown.
5. Cut a tree limb using the brown paper and glue under the oval-shaped owl bodies.
6. Add leaves by tearing small pieces of green paper and gluing them on top of each other.
7. With black scraps, cut and glue eyes on each owl.
8. With yellow scraps, cut and glue feet and beaks on each owl.

Questions for Discussion

What would a baby owl feel like if you could touch it? What shapes did you use to make the body of the owls? What is the difference between painting and printing? Why did you have to print the brown and yellow paint gently over the white paint? How does tearing the green paper make it seem more like the texture of leaves? How are the baby owls you made alike? How are they different?

Share Time/Evaluation

_____

_____

_____

_____

Curriculum Connection

Science, Social Studies, Math, Language Arts, Music, Physical Education

Curriculum Extensions

Science: Learn about owls. Visit a bird sanctuary or invite a speaker in from the Audubon Society or a local bird watching club.

Social Studies: Locate on a map where different types of owls live.

Math: Make up equations by adding and subtracting how many owls are on a limb after some land on the limb or how many fly away.

Language Arts: Read other books about owls. Make up your own story about baby owls.

Music: Sing songs about owls.

Physical Education: With body facing frontward, turn head around as far as you can toward the back. Face front again and turn head the other way as far as possible.

Bear in Two Styles

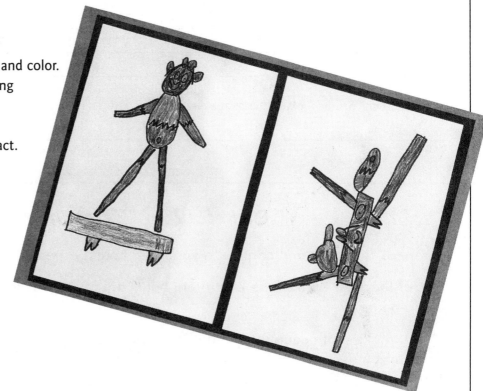

Objectives/Concepts

1. To work with line, shape, and color.
2. To experiment with drawing technique.
3. To create patterns.
4. To experiment with abstract.

Technique

Drawing

Materials

8 in. x 10 in. white paper (2 per student)
12 in. x 18 in. black paper
Black marker
Glue
Colored pencils

Alternate Materials

Colored markers, crayons, colored paper, watercolor paints

Activities/Process

1. Read or give a summary of the book *Bear Party* by William Pene Du Bois, focusing on the illustrations.
2. On one piece of white paper with black marker, draw a bear wearing clothing.
3. Add details and patterns.
4. Discuss that abstract is a style of art that comes from a real object but the visual interpretation has little regard to the realistic impression.
5. On the second piece of white paper, draw the same shapes, designs, and patterns as in the first bear but mix up the arrangement by putting the shapes in different areas. Some can be placed upside down, or even make the parts separate from the whole.
6. Add color with colored pencils.
7. Mat both pieces by gluing them equally spaced on the black paper.

Questions for Discussion

What shapes did you use to make the bear? What clothes or costume is your bear wearing? Where did you use a pattern? What is abstract? How did you abstract your bear drawing?

Share Time/Evaluation

_____

_____

_____

_____

Curriculum Connection

Science, Social Studies, Math, Language Arts, Music, Physical Education

Curriculum Extensions

Science: Compare and contrast a variety of bears, especially the koala bear.

Social Studies: Locate where different bears are found—especially Australia where the koala bears live.

Math: Make math equations using bear counters or bear-shaped cookies. Plan a class party and make cookies by measuring ingredients. Use a bear-shaped cookie cutter.

Language Arts: Read other books about bears. Make up your own story about a bear party. Write and send invitations for a class party. Write a skit about a bear party and act it out. Write bear poems.

Music: Sing songs about bears. Play music and sing songs at a class party.

Physical Education: Learn different kinds of dances for the class party.

Apple Bird

Bird with Apple

Objectives/Concepts

1. To work with shape and color.
2. To experiment with drawing technique.
3. To experiment with painting technique.
4. To experiment with cutting and pasting technique.

Technique

Drawing, Painting, Cutting and Pasting

Materials

12 in. x 18 in. colored paper
4½ in. x 6 in. white paper
8 in. x 10 in. white paper
Crayons
Watercolor paints
Scissors
Glue
¼ in. x 2 in. brown paper

Alternate Materials

Markers, chalk, tempera paint

Activities/Process

1. Read or give a summary of the book *Apple Bird* by Brian Wildsmith, focusing on the illustrations.
2. On 4½ in. x 6 in. white paper with crayons, draw a colorful bird.
3. Cut out the bird.
4. Round the edges of the 8 in. x 10 in. paper to make an apple shape.
5. Paint the apple with watercolor paints.
6. Glue the apple onto the 12 in. x 18 in. colored paper.
7. Glue the bird and the brown stem to the top of the apple.

Questions for Discussion

How did you make an oval shape from a rectangle? What shapes did you use to make the bird? What other colors did you use besides red in your apple and why? What happened when you painted colors next to each other and they were still wet? What is a picture book?

Share Time/Evaluation

_____

_____

_____

_____

Curriculum Connection

Science, Math, Language Arts, Music, Physical Education

Curriculum Extensions

Science: Compare and contrast a variety of apples by noticing the color, shape, size, and taste of each. Discuss the life cycle of an apple from seed to fruit. Make a bird feeder using an apple spread with peanut butter and rolled in birdseed.

Math: Make an apple recipe and measure the ingredients. Estimate how many seeds are in an apple and then count the seeds. Cut an apple into sections for adding and subtracting.

Language Arts: Read other books about apples. Make up your own story about an apple.

Music: Sing songs about birds.

Physical Education: Move around like a bird flying and gliding.

Blanket Design

Objectives/Concepts

1. To work with line, shape, and color.
2. To create layering.
3. To create pattern.
4. To work with symmetry.
5. To experiment with cutting and pasting technique.

Technique

Cutting and Pasting

Materials

12 in. x 18 in. colored paper
6 in. x 9 in. colored paper
12 in. colored paper strips (¼ in., ½ in., 1 in., and
  2 in. thickness)
1 in., 2 in., 3 in., 4 in. colored paper squares
Scissors
Glue
Paper punch
4 in. piece of yarn (4 per student)

Alternate Materials

Markers, crayons (wax or oil), chalk, tempera paint, watercolor paint

Activities/Process

1. Read the book *Ten Little Rabbits* by Virginia Grossman. Focus on the blanket illustrations at the end of the book.
2. Place 6 in. x 9 in. paper in the center of the large colored paper either vertically or horizontally.
3. Do not use glue until the entire design is arranged.
4. Experiment with different designs by placing squares and strips on the paper. Squares can be turned to make diamonds or cut in half to make triangles.

5. Layer some smaller strips or shapes on top of some larger ones. Make sure the design is symmetrical with one side the same as the other and the top the same as the bottom.
6. Once the design is fully arranged, it can be glued.
7. Punch holes in each corner and tie a yarn strip through it for a tassel.

Questions for Discussion

Is your design the same on top and bottom? Is the design the same on both sides? What does symmetrical mean? How did you make a diamond shape from a square? a triangle? Where did you use layering? Why were designs important to the people making the blankets?

Share Time/Evaluation

_____
_____
_____
_____

Curriculum Connection

Science, Social Studies, Math, Language Arts, Music, Physical Education

Curriculum Extensions

Science: Learn about rabbits.

Social Studies: Map out where Native American tribes live. Compare and contrast different living quarters, lifestyles, and customs.

Math: Do some counting from 1 to 10 using subjects other than rabbits. Create various patterns on paper.

Language Arts: Tell a story about what the designs in your blanket could mean. Write a different verse describing rabbits from 1 to 10.

Music: Listen to Native American music. Create the beat of the music by clapping hands or beating drums.

Physical Education: Dance to Native American music keeping step with the beat.

Brown Bear

Objectives/Concepts

1. To work with shape and color.
2. To experiment with printing technique.
3. To experiment with tearing technique.
4. To create texture.
5. To experiment with color mixing.

Technique

Printing, Cutting (Tearing) and Pasting

Materials

12 in. x 18 in. blue paper
9 in. x 12 in. white paper
6 in. x 6 in. white paper
3 in. x 4½ in. white paper (4 per student)
Black paper scraps
2 in. x 2 in. black paper
Tempera paints (red, yellow, and blue)
2 in. x 2 in. sponge
Glue

Alternate Materials

Markers, chalk, crayons, watercolor paint, colored paper, tissue paper

Activities/Process

1. Read or give a summary of the book *Brown Bear, Brown Bear, What Do You See?* by Bill Martin, Jr., focusing on the illustrations.
2. Tear the edges of 9 in. x 12 in. paper to make an oval for the body of a bear.
3. Tear the edges of 6 in. x 6 in. paper to make a circle for the head.

4. Tear all edges of the 3 in. x 4½ in. papers for the legs.
5. Glue the shapes together to form the bear's body. Small scraps can be torn for the ears.
6. Using the sponge piece, mix the primary colors (red, yellow, and blue) to make brown. (Younger children can be given brown paint; older children can mix secondary colors and experiment with using complementary colors to make brown.)
7. Sponge print the brown paint onto the paper bear, giving the texture of fur.
8. Tear a white scrap for the eye and layer with a torn black scrap. Use other black scraps to tear the nose and claws and glue down.

Questions for Discussion

What shapes did you use to make the bear? Why did tearing the paper add to the bear project? Why did you have to tear very slowly? What colors did you use to make brown? Does all the brown look the same? Why not?

Share Time/Evaluation

_____

_____

_____

_____

Curriculum Connection

Science, Social Studies, Math, Language Arts, Music, Physical Education

Curriculum Extensions

Science: Compare and contrast a variety of bears (brown bear, black bear, polar bear, panda bear, koala bear).

Social Studies: Research the different parts of the world where bears live.

Math: Use plastic bear counters or bear-shaped cookies for adding, subtracting, or other math equations.

Language Arts: Read other books about bears. Make up your own story about a bear. Write a bear poem.

Music: Sing bear songs. Put your own bear poems to music.

Physical Education: Play games like tag pretending to be a bear.

Butterfly

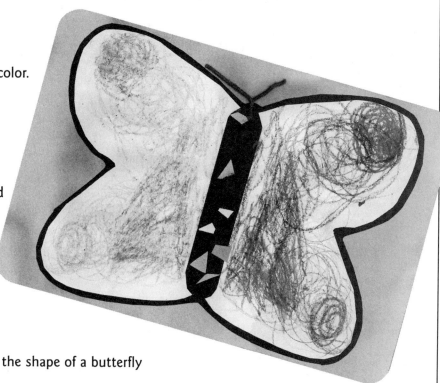

Objectives/Concepts

1. To work with line, shape, and color.
2. To experiment with drawing technique.
3. To create a transfer drawing.
4. To create pattern.
5. To create symmetry.
6. To experiment with cutting and pasting technique.

Technique

Drawing, Cutting and Pasting

Materials

12 in. x 18 in. white paper cut in the shape of a butterfly
2 in. x 12 in. black paper
Colored paper scraps
Oil crayons
Craft stick
Scissors
Glue
Colored pipe cleaner

Alternate Materials

Chalk, tempera paint

Activities/Process

1. Read or give a summary of the book *Look ... a Butterfly* by David Cutts, focusing on the illustrations.
2. On half of the butterfly-shaped paper, with crayons, draw colorful shapes and designs.
3. Fold paper in half and rub over the paper with the craft stick to transfer the image from one half to the other.

4. Color in the shapes and designs on both sides so that they are symmetrical.

5. Round the corners of the black paper and glue down the middle of the butterfly wings.

6. Cut and glue different shapes to make a pattern on the body.

7. Poke a pipe cleaner through the top of the body and twist to make antennae.

Questions for Discussion

What shapes did you use for designs on the butterfly wings? on the butterfly body? How did you get the same design on both butterfly wings?

Share Time/Evaluation

_____

_____

_____

_____

Curriculum Connection

Science, Math, Language Arts, Physical Education

Curriculum Extensions

Science: Compare and contrast a variety of butterflies by noticing the color, shape, and patterns on each. Discuss the life cycle of a butterfly from caterpillar to adult. Observe the life cycle process of the Monarch butterfly.

Math: Make some symmetrical designs. Look for things in nature or manmade that are symmetrical.

Language Arts: Read other books about butterflies. Write a poem about a caterpillar becoming a butterfly.

Physical Education: Crawl like a caterpillar, bend body tightly together as if inside a chrysalis, then extend body and arms to flutter like the wings of a butterfly.

Millions of Cats

Cat

Objectives/Concepts

1. To work with line, shape, and color.
2. To experiment with drawing technique.
3. To experiment with printing.
4. To create texture.
5. To work with pattern.

Technique

Drawing, Printing

Materials

9 in. x 12 in. black paper
8 in. x 11 in. Styrofoam board
Pencil or pen
White printing ink
Brayer (ink roller)
Inking plate

Alternate Materials

Markers, crayons, tempera paint, watercolor paint, colored paper

Activities/Process

1. Read or give a summary of the book *Millions of Cats* by Wanda Ga'g, focusing on the illustrations.
2. On Styrofoam board, draw a large cat making sure the pen or pencil presses in below the surface.
3. Add lines, designs, and patterns to the cat's body.
4. Roll the ink out on the inking plate and then roll the ink on the Styrofoam board.
5. Place the paper onto the Styrofoam board and rub the back of the paper with the palm of your hand.
6. Lift the paper for the image.
7. Rolling the same Styrofoam with more ink and printing on another paper can make more prints. Other color inks or papers can be used.

Questions for Discussion

What is printing? Why does the image come out in reverse? What shapes did you use to make the cat? What happened if you used too much ink? Do you have a favorite pattern on your cat? What kind of lines did you use?

Share Time/Evaluation

_____
_____
_____
_____

Curriculum Connection

Science, Math, Language Arts

Curriculum Extensions

Science: Compare and contrast a variety of cats, noticing the color, shape, and size of each. Visit or invite a pet store owner or someone from the animal shelter to talk about cats. Visit a printing company or the local newspaper to watch the printing process.

Math: Make up math equations using hundreds, thousands, millions, and billions.

Language Arts: Read other books about cats. Make up your own story about a cat. Write a poem about a cat.

Caterpillar

Objectives/Concepts

1. To work with shape and color.
2. To experiment with painting technique.
3. To experiment with cutting and pasting technique.

Technique

Painting, Cutting and Pasting

Materials

9 in. x 12 in. green paper
6 white paper circles about
   2 in. in diameter
Watercolor paints
Scissors
Glue
Scraps of colored paper

Alternate Materials

Markers, crayons, chalk, tempera paint, variety of papers, glitter, printing stamps

Activities/Process

1. Read or give a summary of the book *The Very Hungry Caterpillar* by Eric Carle, focusing on the illustrations.
2. Paint the white circles, trying out different watercolor painting techniques such as wet on wet and dry brush.
3. Glue the circles together forming the body of a caterpillar.
4. With colored paper scraps, make the head and facial features of a caterpillar and glue it onto the painted body.
5. Add legs, antennae, and other details to the caterpillar.

6. Cut the 9 in. x 12 in. green paper into a pointed oval shape for a leaf.
7. Cut or tear a small piece away from the leaf as if the caterpillar had eaten into it.
8. Glue the caterpillar onto the leaf.

Questions for Discussion

What happened when you painted colors next to each other and they were still wet? What happened when you used little amounts of water on dry paper? How did you change colors from dark to light? How did you make both eyes and antennae the same size and shape? How did you make the form of the caterpillar's body?

Share Time/Evaluation

_____

_____

_____

_____

Curriculum Connection

Science, Math, Language Arts, Music, Physical Education

Curriculum Extensions

Science: Compare and contrast a variety of caterpillars by the color, shape, size, and texture of each. Discuss the life cycle of a caterpillar, from tiny egg to adult moth or butterfly. Keep a caterpillar in the classroom and watch it eat.

Math: Make different caterpillars by using different amounts of circles. Make a caterpillar using different patterns. Use the circles of caterpillar bodies for adding and subtracting.

Language Arts: Read other books about caterpillars. Make up your own story about a caterpillar. Make a caterpillar from an old sock and act out a story.

Music: Move your body or a caterpillar puppet to the beat of music.

Physical Education: Pretend that you are a caterpillar and move around the room.

Chameleons Are Cool

Chameleon

Objectives/Concepts

1. To work with line, shape, and color.
2. To experiment with drawing technique.
3. To experiment with painting technique.
4. To experiment with printing technique.
5. To create texture.
6. To create pattern.
7. To experiment with color blending.
8. To experiment with crayon resist.

Technique

Drawing, Painting, Printing

Materials

12 in. x 18 in. white paper
Crayons
Watercolor paints
Q-tips

Alternate Materials

Markers, chalk, tempera paint, colored paper

Activities/Process

1. Read or give a summary of the book *Chameleons Are Cool* by Martin Jenkins, focusing on the illustrations.
2. On white paper draw a large oval for a chameleon's body. Add a triangle shaped head, legs, and a tail.

3. Draw eyes, mouth, horns, spikes, and other individual details.
4. Crayons can be used to make some circles on the body for texture.
5. Paint in with watercolor paints, blending colors and making patterns.
6. On dry paint areas, print some dots using Q-tips dipped in the wet watercolor cakes.

Questions for Discussion

What shapes did you use to make the chameleon? What happened when you painted colors next to each other and they were still wet? How did you show texture? What is the difference between painting and printing? Where did you use a pattern? What is crayon resist? What is camouflage?

Share Time/Evaluation

_____

_____

_____

_____

Curriculum Connection

Science, Social Studies, Math, Language Arts, Physical Education

Curriculum Extensions

Science: Learn about chameleons. Compare and contrast a variety of lizards. Learn about reptiles. Invite someone from a pet store to bring in a chameleon. Keep a chameleon in an aquarium in the classroom. Discuss other animals whose skin or fur helps to camouflage them.

Social Studies: Learn where chameleons live and locate on a map.

Math: Use dots to make math equations. Try some different kinds of patterns. Estimate how many dots are on the chameleon artwork and count them.

Language Arts: Read other books about chameleons. Make up your own story about a chameleon. Pretend that you are a chameleon and describe when you change color.

Physical Education: Play hide-and-seek. Play tag wearing different color pinnies. You can tag only those people wearing the same color. Keep changing pinny colors.

City Buildings

Objectives/Concepts

1. To work with line and shape.
2. To experiment with cutting and pasting technique.
3. To work with positive and negative shape.
4. To work with horizontal and vertical line.
5. To create silhouette.

Technique

Cutting and Pasting

Materials

12 in. x 18 in. white paper
12 in. x 18 in. black paper
¼ in. x 12 in. white paper (a few per student)
Scissors
Glue

Alternate Materials

Tempera paint, Styrofoam sheet, ink, inking plate, roller, printing paper

Activities/Process

1. Read or give a summary of the book *Round Trip* by Ann Jonas, focusing on the illustrations.
2. Using the black paper, cut horizontal and vertical lines to create several attached silhouetted buildings.
3. Glue to the white paper.
4. Cut small squares using the ¼ white strip and glue them on to the buildings for windows.

Questions for Discussion

Which way is horizontal and which way is vertical? What is a positive shape? What is a negative shape?

Explain why if we hold the paper the way we glued it, it looks like silhouetted buildings with lights on, but if we turn the paper upside down it looks like white buildings with stars in a black sky.

Share Time/Evaluation

_____

_____

_____

_____

Curriculum Connection

Science, Social Studies, Math, Language Arts, Music

Curriculum Extensions

Science: Learn about optical illusions and look at other examples.

Social Studies: Locate large cities and look at the buildings. Discuss city life.

Math: See how many squares you can cut from different lengths of paper cut in different size widths.

Language Arts: Read other books about cities. Write a descriptive paragraph about a city at night.

Music: Learn songs about cities.

Clay Dragon

Objectives/Concepts

1. To work with line, shape, and color.
2. To experiment with sculpture.
3. To experiment with painting technique.
4. To work in three-dimension.
5. To experiment with clay.
6. To create texture.

Technique

Sculpture

Materials

Self-hardening clay about the size of a
   tennis ball
Pencil or wooden stick
Tempera paints

Alternate Materials

Plasticine clay, watercolor paints, papier-mâché

Activities/Process

1. Read or give a summary of the book *The Popcorn Dragon* by Jane Thayer, focusing on the illustrations.
2. Divide the ball of clay so that one piece is twice as big as the other piece.
3. Roll the large piece into a fat coil. Lift the front part and shape into a snakelike creature.
4. With the other clay, add legs, wings, horns, spikes, and other details.
5. Add texture with the pencil or wooden stick.
6. Either allow the clay to dry before painting or paint then allow the clay to dry.

Questions for Discussion

What is a coil? How did you attach the wings? What would happen if the pieces of clay that are added to the coil are too thin? How does it look like the dragon would feel? Why was the dragon in the story called the Popcorn Dragon?

Share Time/Evaluation

_____

_____

_____

_____

Curriculum Connection

Science, Social Studies, Math, Language Arts, Music, Physical Education

Curriculum Extensions

Science: Compare and contrast different kinds of clay and do some experiments on what happens to clay in water, in the sun, in the air, and so on. Research popcorn to see how it grows, how it is harvested, how it is manufactured, and why it pops.

Social Studies: Learn the myths behind dragons. Compare and contrast the medieval European and the Asian dragons.

Math: Estimate how much popcorn is in a jar. Do math equations using popcorn. Measure the length and width of a coiled piece of self-hardening clay before and after it dries. Do the same with oil-based plasticine clay and compare the results.

Language Arts: Read other books about dragons. Make up your own story about a dragon. Write a paragraph on why it is not a good thing to show off.

Music: Listen to and learn songs about dragons.

Physical Education: Pretend to be a kernel of corn, squat low to the floor, and jump up as if you were popping.

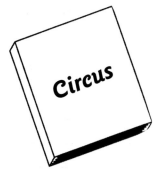

Clown

Objectives/Concepts

1. To work with line, shape, and color.
2. To experiment with drawing technique.
3. To create pattern.
4. To create texture.
5. To experiment with expression.

Technique

Drawing

Materials

6 in. x 18 in. white paper
Markers
½ in. or 1 in. precut circles (6 per student)
Glue

Alternate Materials

Crayons, colored paper, self-stick coding label dots, yarn, pom-poms, material scraps

Activities/Process

1. Read or give a summary of the book *Circus* by Brian Wildsmith, focusing on the illustrations.
2. On white paper with markers, draw a clown with long legs. Position the arms stretched out to the sides as if to juggle.
3. Make the face of the clown either happy, sad, surprised, or another emotion.
4. Color in with lots of patterns.
5. Glue the circles in a curved fashion spaced from one hand around the head to the other hand.

Questions for Discussion

Why do you think the legs of the clown are so long? What shapes did you use in your patterns? What patterns did you make? What makes it look like the clown is juggling? What expression did you put on your clown's face?

Share Time/Evaluation

_____

_____

_____

_____

Curriculum Connection

Science, Social Studies, Math, Language Arts, Music, Physical Education

Curriculum Extensions

Science: Learn about gravity.

Social Studies: Invite a clown into the classroom.

Math: Make up math equations using circles. Count how many times you can toss a ball in the air without it dropping.

Language Arts: Read other books about clowns. Make up your own story about a clown. Put on a play about a circus. Write a poem about a clown or the circus. Write a paragraph about feelings and what makes us feel differently.

Music: Listen to circus music.

Physical Education: Try walking on stilts. Practice juggling.

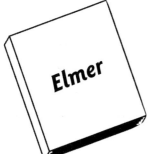

Elmer

Colorful Elephant

Objectives/Concepts

1. To work with shape and color.
2. To experiment with drawing technique.
3. To experiment with cutting and pasting technique.
4. To work with overlapping.

Technique

Drawing, Cutting and Pasting

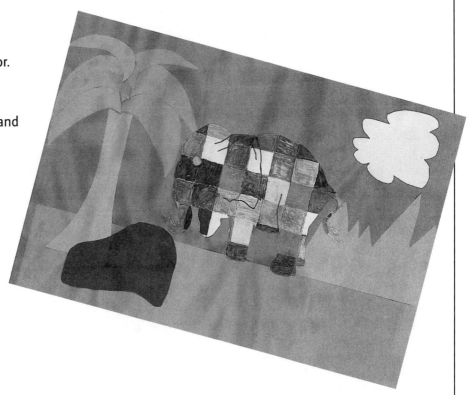

Materials

12 in. x 18 in. blue paper
8½ in. x 11 in. white paper with a 1 in. grid
Markers
Colored paper scraps
Scissors
Glue
Pencil

Alternate Materials

Crayons, colored pencils, tempera paint, watercolor paint

Activities/Process

1. Read or give a summary of the book *Elmer* by David McKee, focusing on the illustrations.
2. With pencil on the back side of the grid paper, draw a large elephant.
3. Cut the elephant out and color in the grids with various colored markers.
4. Add an eye and or other details with colored paper.
5. Using colored paper, make a jungle scene with trees, flowers, a lake, or other landscape features and glue on the blue paper.
6. Glue the colored elephant onto the scene.

Questions for Discussion

What shapes did you use to make the elephant? How can we tell that the elephant is closer to us than parts of the jungle? Why did you choose to put the colors where you did on the elephant?

Share Time/Evaluation

_____

_____

_____

_____

Curriculum Connection

Science, Social Studies, Math, Language Arts, Physical Education

Curriculum Extensions

Science: Compare and contrast elephants from different areas. Discuss a jungle environment.

Social Studies: Look up different areas where elephants live and learn about the geographical areas. Find out where there are jungles.

Math: Use different types of graph paper to graph mathematical information.

Language Arts: Read other books about elephants. Make up your own story about Elmer the elephant.

Physical Education: Do the elephant walk by putting one hand on the floor and the other arm up by your face like an elephant's trunk and walk with both legs and one hand touching the floor alternately. Play elephant tag.

Fish
Eyes

Colorful Patterned Fish

Objectives/Concepts

1. To work with line, shape, and color.
2. To experiment with cutting and pasting technique.
3. To create pattern.
4. To work with layering.

Technique

Cutting and Pasting

Materials

12 in. x 18 in. dark blue paper
12 in. x 18 in. colored paper
Colored paper scraps
Scissors
Glue
Paper punch

Alternate Materials

Markers, chalk, tempera paint, watercolor paint, paper varieties, shape stickers, glitter

Activities/Process

1. Read or give a summary of the book *Fish Eyes* by Lois Ehlert, focusing on the illustrations.
2. Cut a large oval for the fish body from the large colored paper. This can be a fat or thin oval that is straight or somewhat curved.
3. Add some kind of triangular tail and triangular or oval fins of different colors.
4. Add details, designs, and patterns by layering colors, cutting lines and shapes, and punching circles.
5. Glue the fish to the blue paper.

Questions for Discussion

What shapes did you use to make the fish? Where did you layer paper? What patterns did you make? What did you do to make more than one line or shape the same?

Share Time/Evaluation

_____

_____

_____

_____

Curriculum Connection

Science, Social Studies, Math, Language Arts, Music, Physical Education

Curriculum Extensions

Science: Compare and contrast a variety of fish by noticing the color, shape, and size of each. Keep an aquarium in the classroom. Visit or invite a speaker in from a fish hatchery.

Social Studies: Locate areas where tropical fish would be found.

Math: Use fish-shaped crackers to do math equations. Write some numbers on cutout fish, put a paper clip on each fish, and with a magnet attached to a string on the end of a stick, go fishing to make up math equations.

Language Arts: Read other books about fish. Make up your own story about a big catch or the fish that got away. Write a paragraph describing the beautiful fish you would see while scuba diving.

Music: Sing songs about fish.

Physical Education: Using a magnetic fishing pole, fish for objects and release them in a different area. Move around as if you were a fish swimming.

Constellations

Objectives/Concepts

1. To work with shape.
2. To work with contour.
3. To work with silhouette.
4. To work with repetition.
5. To experiment with drawing technique.
6. To experiment with cutting and pasting technique.

Technique

Drawing, Cutting and Pasting

Materials

12 in. x 18 in. black paper
12 in. x 18 in. dark blue paper
Paper scraps (yellow, white)
Paper punch (circle, star)
Pencil
Scissors
Glue

Alternate Materials

Tempera paint (white, yellow), Q-tip, star stamp, stick on stars

Activities/Process

1. Read or give a summary of the book *The Night Sky* by Alice Pernick, focusing on the illustrations.
2. On dark blue paper, draw the contour of a large animal, person, or object.
3. Cut it out.
4. Glue the shape onto the black paper.
5. Punch circles and stars from white and yellow paper and glue them inside and outside the silhouette shape, making sure that some of them are part of the contour.

Questions for Discussion

What is a star? What gives a star its shape? What is a constellation? Why do you think there are constellations? What makes some stars seem brighter than others? What makes some stars seem bigger than others? Why do the positions of stars seem to change?

Share Time/Evaluation

_____

_____

_____

_____

Curriculum Connection

Science, Math, Language Arts, Music

Curriculum Extensions

Science: Visit a planetarium. Watch the night sky for a week or month and note what you see. Look at star charts and try to locate constellations. Research the names of constellations.

Math: Using star-shaped objects, figure out mathematical equations.

Language Arts: Read other books about stars. Make up your own constellation, give it a name, and write a story about it. Read some Greek literature about some of the constellation names. Write a poem about stars.

Music: Listen to some music about stars. Sing songs about stars.

Crazy Quilt

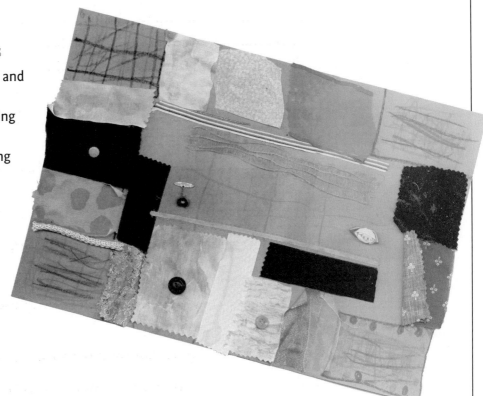

Objectives/Concepts

1. To work with line, shape, and color.
2. To experiment with drawing technique.
3. To experiment with cutting and pasting technique.
4. To create pattern.
5. To create overlapping.

Technique

Drawing, Cutting and Pasting

Materials

9 in. x 12 in. colored paper
8 in. x 10 in. white paper
Crayons
2 in. x 3 in. wallpaper varieties
2 in. x 2 in. pieces of patterned material
    (edges should be cut with pinking shears)
3 in. pieces of ribbon, lace, and other trims
Scissors
Glue
Buttons

Alternate Materials

Markers, colored pencils, colored paper varieties, gift wrapping paper

Activities/Process

1. Read or give a summary of the book *The Quilt Story* by Tony Johnston, focusing on the illustrations.

2. On white paper with black crayon, make some straight, horizontal, vertical, and diagonal lines to divide the space into smaller squares, rectangles, trapezoids, and other areas to resemble little pieces of material sewn together in quilt fashion.
3. With colored crayons, decorate each space with patterns.
4. Glue a few pieces of material, wallpaper, and ribbon or trims over the drawing.
5. Glue one or two buttons on the drawing.
6. Add a few small black lines around the wallpaper and material to look like stitches.

Questions for Discussion

What is a quilt? What shapes did you use in your quilt? What are some of the patterns you created? Did you ever use the same pattern more than once? What is your favorite pattern?

Share Time/Evaluation

_____
_____
_____
_____

Curriculum Connection

Social Studies, Math, Language Arts

Curriculum Extensions

Social Studies: Learn about the history of quilts. Find out about quilting as a colonial craft and learn more about colonial times.

Math: Make various paper quilts or color in graph paper for quilting designs and do mathematical equations based on the quilts.

Language Arts: Read other books about quilts. Make up your own story about the meaning behind a quilt. Interview older relatives to find out stories of the past and keep a journal.

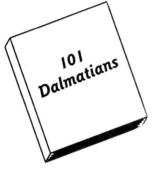

Dalmatian

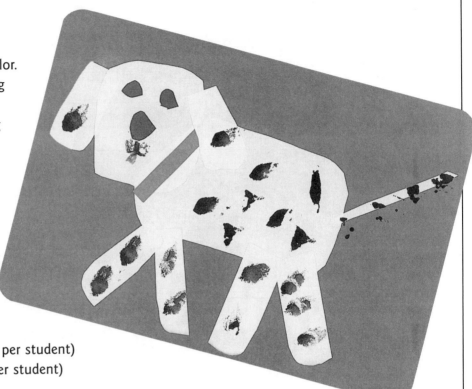

Objectives/Concepts

1. To work with shape and color.
2. To experiment with printing technique.
3. To experiment with cutting and pasting technique.
4. To create pattern.

Technique

Printing, Cutting and Pasting

Materials

9 in. x 12 in. white paper
6 in. x 6 in. white paper
4½ in. x 6 in. white paper (2 per student)
2 in. x 9 in. white paper (4 per student)
1 in. x 9 in. red paper
Black paper scraps
Black tempera paint
Scissors
Glue
1 in. x 2 in. sponge

Alternate Materials

Markers, crayons, white tempera paint

Activities/Process

1. Read or give a summary of the book *101 Dalmatians* adapted by Justine Korman, focusing on the illustrations.
2. Round the corners of the 9 in. x 12 in. rectangle to make an oval for the body.
3. Round the corners of the 6 in. square to make a circle for the head and glue it to the body.
4. Glue on the four white strips for the legs.
5. Round the edges of the 4½ in. x 6 in. paper and glue onto the head for ears.
6. Cut a tail from some white scraps.

7. Using the sponge and black paint, print spots onto the dog.
8. Cut eyes and nose from black scraps.
9. Glue the red strip on the dog's neck for a collar and cut to fit.

Questions for Discussion

What shapes did you use to make the dog? How did you make an oval shape from a rectangle? What shape was the circle before you rounded the edges to make it a circle? What is printing and how is it different from painting?

Share Time/Evaluation

_____

_____

_____

_____

Curriculum Connection

Science, Social Studies, Math, Language Arts, Music, Physical Education

Curriculum Extensions

Science: Compare and contrast a variety of dogs. Learn about Dalmatians. Invite someone in from a pet store to explain the care of puppies. Check pet stores, animal shelters, or local fire departments to see if they have a Dalmatian the children could see. Learn about animation.

Social Studies: Locate London (where the story takes place) on a map. Learn about London.

Math: Count to 101. Bring in 101 different items, such as 101 toothpicks, 101 candies, 101 buttons, or the like. Make a necklace out of 101 ringed cereal pieces.

Language Arts: Read other books about Dalmatians. Make up your own story about 101 of something. Come up with 101 names for the puppies. Write a story about what took place after the Dalmatians moved to a farm.

Music: Listen to piano music. Listen to the soundtrack of *101 Dalmatians*.

Physical Education: Take 101 baby steps and then giant steps to see where you end up. Do different activities to see if you can get up to 101 times (e.g., bouncing a ball, skipping, jumping rope). Play tag with one person as Cruella and the rest as the Dalmatian puppies.

Dragon

Objectives/Concepts

1. To work with line, shape, and color.
2. To experiment with drawing technique.
3. To experiment with painting technique.
4. To experiment with crayon resist.
5. To create texture.
6. To mix and blend colors.

Technique

Drawing, Painting

Materials

12 in. x 18 in. white drawing paper
Black crayon
Watercolor paints

Alternate Materials

Crayons, colored pencils, chalk, tempera paints

Activities/Process

1. Read or give a summary of the book *The Popcorn Dragon* by Jane Thayer, focusing on the illustrations.
2. With black crayon, draw a simple body shape, large enough to fill the page.
3. Add a long pointed tail, feet, claws, wings, horns, and other details.
4. Make scales on the body and textured lines on the skin.
5. Add smoke coming from the nostrils and fire from the mouth.
6. Paint in with watercolor paints.

Questions for Discussion

Does your dragon look scary or playful and why? How did you show texture? What shapes did you use to make the dragon? What happened when the paints went over the crayon? Did you blend any colors? What colors did you make from other colors?

Share Time/Evaluation

_____

_____

_____

_____

Curriculum Connection

Science, Social Studies, Math, Language Arts, Music, Physical Education

Curriculum Extensions

Science: Research popcorn to see how it grows, how it is harvested, how it is manufactured, and why it pops.

Social Studies: Learn the myths behind dragons. Compare and contrast the medieval European and the Asian dragons.

Math: Estimate how much popcorn is in a jar. Do math equations using popcorn.

Language Arts: Read other books about dragons. Make up your own story about a dragon. Write a paragraph on why it is not a good thing to show off.

Music: Listen to and learn songs about dragons.

Physical Education: Pretend to be a kernel of corn, squat low to the floor, and jump up as if you were popping.

 **The Ant and the Elephant**

Elephant

Objectives/Concepts

1. To work with shape and form.
2. To work with clay as a medium.
3. To create three-dimension.
4. To experiment with sculpture.
5. To create texture.

Technique

Sculpture

Materials

Clay (earth clay or plasticine clay)
Pencil or pointed wooden craft stick

Alternate Materials

Papier-mâché

Activities/Process

1. Read or give a summary of the book *The Ant and the Elephant* by Bill Peet, focusing on the illustrations.
2. Divide the ball of clay into two pieces, one piece twice as big as the other piece.
3. Roll the larger piece of clay into an oval shape resembling a potato.
4. With the pencil or wooden stick, draw a horizontal and a vertical line making a plus sign across the clay, cutting slightly below the surface.
5. Pinch and pull the four sections of clay to make four short, fat cylinder-shaped legs coming away from the body.
6. Divide the second ball of clay into two pieces. Roll one piece into a circle or oval for the head and attach it to the body.
7. Divide the rest of the clay into three pieces. Roll one piece into a coil and attach to the head as a trunk.
8. Flatten the last two pieces into slabs and attach as the ears.

9. Details such as tusks and tail can be pinched and pulled from the clay, and the eyes can be rolled or drawn with the pencil.
10. Texture of the elephant skin can be drawn with the pencil or stick.

Discussion

How does the clay feel? What is three-dimensional? What is the difference between shape and form? What would happen if the legs were too long or thin? Why do you need to make sure the head is smoothed onto the body so that it becomes one piece of clay? How did you make a coil? How did you make a slab? How did you make texture?

Share Time/Evaluation

_____
_____
_____
_____

Curriculum Connection

Science, Social Studies, Math, Language Arts, Physical Education

Curriculum Extensions

Science: Compare and contrast elephants from different geographical areas. Observe ants in an ant farm.

Social Studies: Look up the different areas where elephants live and learn about the geographical areas.

Math: With balls of clay, make up different mathematical equations. Use raisins for ants and make up math equations, then eat the raisins.

Language Arts: Read other books about elephants and ants. Make up your own story about animals or people helping each other. Tell a story about someone doing a good deed. Put on a play about the elephant and the ant.

Physical Education: Do the elephant walk by putting one hand on the floor and the other arm up by your face like an elephant's trunk and walk with both legs and one hand touching the floor alternately. Play elephant tag.

Fall Leaves

Objectives/Concepts

1. To work with line, shape, and color.
2. To experiment with drawing technique.
3. To experiment with painting technique.
4. To experiment with crayon resist.
5. To create overlapping.

Technique

Drawing, Painting

Materials

12 in. x 18 in. white paper
Crayons (wax or oil)
Watercolor paints
Leaves or precut stencils of leaves

Alternate Materials

Markers, chalk, tempera, paint

Activities/Process

1. Read or give a summary of the book *Fall Leaves Fall* by Zoe Hall, focusing on the illustrations.
2. On 12 in. x 18 in. white paper with crayons, trace the outline of a variety of leaves. Make sure that some overlap. Different leaves can be traced in the different fall colors.
3. Add the lines for the veins to the leaves.
4. Paint each leaf one color with watercolor paints, using the different fall colors.
5. Paint the area around the leaves with a variety of any colors allowing the colors to blend together.

Questions for Discussion

Why do leaves change color? What do you notice about leaves from different kinds of trees? What are the lines on leaves called and what function do they have? What happened when you painted colors next to each other and they were still wet? Where did you overlap? Which leaves are on top of other leaves?

Share Time/Evaluation

_____

_____

_____

_____

Curriculum Connection

Science, Social Studies, Math, Language Arts, Physical Education

Curriculum Extensions

Science: Compare and contrast a variety of leaves by noticing the color, shape, and size of each. Look at leaves through a magnifying glass or microscope. Go on a scavenger hunt looking for different leaves. Press and label leaves.

Social Studies: On a large map, chart where different trees exist.

Math: Sort leaves by shape, color, and/or size. Estimate how many seeds are in a pile. Go on a walk and chart how many of what kind of trees were seen.

Language Arts: Read other books about leaves. Write a poem about leaves. Tell or write an imaginary story about why leaves change color.

Physical Education: Pretend that you are a leaf and float in the wind, turning and falling gently to the ground.

Fall Tree

Objectives/Concepts

1. To work with line, shape, and color.
2. To experiment with drawing technique.
3. To experiment with cutting and pasting technique.
4. To create color blends.
5. To work with overlapping.
6. To work with silhouette.

Technique

Drawing, Cutting and Pasting

Materials

9 in. x 12 in. white paper
9 in. x 12 in. black paper
2 in. x 2 in. tissue paper (several each of red, yellow, and orange)
Glue (both regular and watered down)
Paste brush
Scissors

Alternate Materials

Oil crayons, chalk, tempera paint, watercolor paint

Activities/Process

1. Read or give a summary of the book *A Tree Is Nice* by Janice May Udry, focusing on the illustrations.
2. On black paper, draw and cut out a large tree with branches but no leaves.
3. Paint some watered down glue on the white paper. Add squares of tissue paper making sure to overlap edges and then paint a layer of watered down glue on top of the tissue paper. Fill in all spaces on the white paper.
4. Glue the silhouette of the tree on top of the tissue paper.

Questions for Discussion

What are the warm colors? How do they make us feel? What happened when you put colors on top of each other? What is silhouette? Why do leaves change color in the fall in certain climates?

Share Time/Evaluation

_____

_____

_____

_____

Curriculum Connection

Science, Social Studies, Math, Language Arts, Music

Curriculum Extensions

Science: Compare and contrast a variety of trees and leaves by noticing the color, shape, and size of each. Collect leaves from different trees. Go on a walking field trip and notice the trees. Plant a tree.

Social Studies: Find out in what geographical areas the leaves on trees change color. Find out what kind of trees grow in what geographical areas.

Math: Gather different leaves, chart them, and do some mathematical equations using the leaves. Measure leaves.

Language Arts: Read other books about trees. Read and write some poetry about trees. Write your own story as to why a tree is nice.

Music: Listen to and sing some songs about trees.

Flowers in Vase

Objectives/Concepts

1. To work with line, shape, and color.
2. To experiment with drawing technique.
3. To experiment with cutting and pasting technique.
4. To create pattern.
5. To create overlapping.

Technique

Drawing, Cutting and Pasting

Materials

12 in. x 18 in. colored paper
8 in. x 10 in. white paper
Colored markers
Scraps of colored paper
2 in. x 6 in. paper (several varieties of green)
Glue

Alternate Materials

Crayons, chalk, tempera paint, watercolor paint,
paper varieties

Activities/Process

1. Read or give a summary of the book *Alison's Zinnia* by Anita Lobel, focusing on the illustrations.
2. Fold white paper in half and on outside edge, away from the fold, draw the contour edge of a vase.
3. Cut on the line making sure not to cut the fold.
4. Open the vase and decorate it with colored markers to make designs and patterns.
5. With colored paper scraps, cut shapes to make a variety of flowers.
6. Cut stems from the green strips and glue to the flowers.
7. Arrange the flowers and stems in the vase so that some overlap others.
8. Glue down.

Questions for Discussion

How did you make the petals on a flower the same size and shape? What shapes did you use to make the petals on the flowers? Where did you overlap? How are flowers similar? How are flowers different?

Share Time/Evaluation

_____

_____

_____

_____

Curriculum Connection

Science, Social Studies, Math, Language Arts

Curriculum Extensions

Science: Compare and contrast a variety of flowers by noticing the color, shape, and size of each. Discuss the life cycle of a flower. Draw a flower and label its parts. Make a flower garden or plant some seeds in small containers and watch them grow.

Social Studies: Look up where different flowers grow geographically.

Math: Estimate how many seeds are in a package, then count them before planting. Use petals for adding and subtracting. Measure the height of flowers as they grow. Make charts to compare favorite flowers or chart flowers by color.

Language Arts: Read other books and poetry about flowers. Write a paragraph describing how to plant a flower garden. Write your own poems about flowers. Pretend that you are a bug and describe your journey on a flower.

Flying Bird

Objectives/Concepts

1. To work with line, shape, and color.
2. To experiment with contour line.
3. To experiment with painting technique.
4. To experiment with cutting and pasting technique.
5. To work with primary colors.

Technique

Painting, Cutting and Pasting

Materials

12 in. x 18 in. white paper
6 in. x 9 in. variety of colored papers
Scissors
Glue
Tempera paint (red, yellow, blue)

Alternate Materials

Crayons, markers, chalk, paper varieties, feathers

Activities/Process

1. Read or give a summary of the book *The Mountain That Loved a Bird* by Alice McLerran, focusing on the illustrations.
2. With colored paper, cut an oval for the body, a circle for the head, triangles for the tail and wings, and glue onto the white paper.
3. Add eye and beak with colored paper.
4. With yellow paint, paint a thick line around the contour of the bird.
5. Paint a thick red line around the yellow line also following the contour.
6. Paint the rest of the paper blue.

Questions for Discussion

What shapes did you use to make the bird? How did you make an oval shape from a rectangle? What are the three primary colors and why are they important colors? What is a contour edge?

Share Time/Evaluation

_____

_____

_____

_____

Curriculum Connection

Science, Social Studies, Math, Language Arts, Music, Physical Education

Curriculum Extensions

Science: Compare and contrast a variety of birds by noticing the color, shape, and size of each. Make a bird feeder using an apple spread with peanut butter and rolled in birdseed.

Social Studies: Find mountain ranges on a world map. Note different birds from different geographical areas.

Math: Estimate some birdseed in a container. Use large birdseed for adding and subtracting. Make charts about birds.

Language Arts: Read other books about birds. Make up your own story about a bird. Write a poem about a bird. Write a story or poem about a mountain. Tell a story about something or someone caring for something else.

Music: Sing songs about birds.

Physical Education: Move around like a bird flying or gliding.

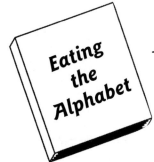

Eating the Alphabet

Fruit and Vegetable Still Life

Objectives/Concepts

1. To work with shape and color.
2. To experiment with drawing technique.
3. To experiment with cutting and pasting technique.
4. To create texture.
5. To create a three-dimensional effect.
6. To work with overlapping.
7. To work with size relationship (proportion).
8. To experiment with color blending.

Technique

Drawing, Cutting and Pasting

Materials

12 in. x 18 in. colored paper
6 in. x 6 in. tan paper
4½ in. x 6 in. colored paper varieties
Chalk
Brown crayon
Scissors
Glue
Textured material

Alternate Materials

Crayons, watercolor paints

Activities/Process

1. Read or give a summary of the book E*ating the Alphabet* by Lois Ehlert, focusing on the illustrations.
2. Round the two bottom corners of the tan paper to make a basket.
3. Put a textured material under the tan paper and rub over it with the brown crayon creating a texture rubbing.

4. Cut a variety of fruits and vegetables from the colored papers.

5. With colored chalk, add color details, highlights, and shadows to the fruits and vegetables.

6. Arrange the fruits and vegetables so that some will be in the basket and some will be around the basket. Glue down.

Questions for Discussion

How did you make the texture of the basket? What shapes did you use for some of the fruits and vegetables? What other colors did you use besides red in your apple and why? What makes the fruits and vegetables seem like they are three-dimensional? Where did you overlap and what does that show?

Share Time/Evaluation

_____

_____

_____

_____

Curriculum Connection

Science, Social Studies, Math, Language Arts

Curriculum Extensions

Science: Compare and contrast a variety of fruits by noticing the color, shape, size, and taste of each. Discuss the life cycle of fruits and vegetables from seed to maturity. Plant a garden. Visit a farmer's garden. Perform different experiments using fruits and vegetables.

Social Studies: Locate where various fruits and vegetables are grown, where they are native to, and the type of climate they need.

Math: Cut various fruits into sections for adding and subtracting; make a fruit salad when finished. Make various charts, such as favorite fruits and vegetables or fruits and vegetables by color.

Language Arts: Read other books about fruits and vegetables. Make up your own garden story. Write poems about different fruits or vegetables. Make an alphabet book naming different fruits and vegetables for the letters.

Gingerbread Man

Objectives/Concepts

1. To work with line, shape, and color.
2. To experiment with drawing technique.
3. To experiment with painting technique.
4. To experiment with cutting and pasting technique.
5. To create pattern.
6. To work with symmetry.

Technique

Drawing, Painting, Cutting and Pasting

Materials

12 in. x 18 in. light brown paper, precut in the shape of a gingerbread man
Colored paper scraps
Colored chalk
White tempera paint
Scissors (straight-edged and fancy-edged)
Glue
2 in. x 3 in. tissue paper

Alternate Materials

Markers, crayons, tempera paint, candies, raisins, lace, trim, buttons

Activities/Process

1. Read or give a summary of the book *The Gingerbread Man*, focusing on the illustrations by Bonnie and Bill Rutherford.
2. On the gingerbread man–shaped paper, make lines and patterns by dipping the chalk into white paint and drawing. Dip the chalk frequently.
3. Add eyes and details with colored paper, using a variety of edged scissors.

4. Make the designs symmetrical so that both sides of the gingerbread man are the same.

5. Pinch and twist the middle of the tissue paper and glue it down to make a bow.

Questions for Discussion

What kinds of lines did you use? Where did you make a pattern? What happened when you dipped the chalk into the paint and drew with it? Are both sides of the gingerbread boy decorated the same way?

Share Time/Evaluation

_____

_____

_____

_____

Curriculum Connection

Science, Social Studies, Math, Language Arts, Music, Physical Education

Curriculum Extensions

Science: Discuss the parts of the body. Discuss what the different animals would naturally eat.

Social Studies: Map out different areas in the community to which the gingerbread man could run. To introduce young children to the school building, the teacher could hide gingerbread man cookies somewhere in the school and the children could walk around looking for him. Go on a walk around the school grounds looking for the gingerbread man.

Math: Make gingerbread man cookies and measure the ingredients. Estimate how many small gingerbread man cookies are in a jar. Using small store-bought gingerbread cookies do math equations.

Language Arts: Read other versions of the gingerbread man, compare and contrast. Make up your own story about a gingerbread man. Act out a skit or make a puppet show about the gingerbread man.

Music: Sing the gingerbread man song.

Physical Education: Play tag by trying to catch someone pretending to be the gingerbread man.

Giraffe with Neckties

Objectives/Concepts

1. To work with line, shape, and color.
2. To experiment with drawing technique.
3. To experiment with cutting and pasting.
4. To create with pattern.
5. To create with texture.

Technique

Drawing, Cutting and Pasting

Materials

6 in. x 9 in. yellow paper
4½ in. x 6 in. yellow paper
2 in. x 6 in. yellow paper
1 in. x 4 in. yellow paper (4 per student)
1 in. x 6 in. black paper
Black paper scraps
1 in. x 4 in. white paper (several pieces per student)
½ in. x 3 in. white paper (several per student)
Markers

Alternate Materials

Crayons, white paper, tempera paints, watercolor paints

Activities/Process

1. Read or give a summary of the book *Animals Should Definitely Not Wear Clothing* by Judi Barrett, focusing on the illustrations.
2. Round the corners of the 6 in. x 9 in. and 4½ in. x 6 in. yellow papers and glue one on each end of the 2 in. x 6 in. paper for the body and head of a giraffe.
3. Glue the 1 in. strips on for the legs.
4. Glue the black strip to the neck for the mane. This can be cut or fringed for texture.

5. Use black scraps to make eyes, nose, hooves, and markings on the fur.
6. With the 1 in. white strips, cut the two bottom corners off at a diagonal and round the two top corners. Glue one ½ in. strip at a diagonal to the top right-hand side.
7. With colored markers, draw designs or patterns to decorate the neckties. Make several different neckties.
8. Glue the neckties to the giraffe's neck.

Questions for Discussion

How did you make an oval shape from a rectangle? What shapes did you use to make the giraffe? What patterns did you use in your neckties? Should all the markings on the giraffe's body be the same? Why?

Share Time/Evaluation

_____
_____
_____
_____

Curriculum Connection

Science, Social Studies, Math, Language Arts

Curriculum Extensions

Science: Research giraffes.

Social Studies: Find where giraffes live and locate on a map.

Math: Work with different shapes and patterns.

Language Arts: Read other books about giraffes. Make up your own story or write a poem about a giraffe wearing clothing.

Hand Design

Objectives/Concepts

1. To work with line, shape, and color.
2. To experiment with drawing technique.
3. To experiment with cutting and pasting technique.
4. To create design.
5. To create pattern.

Technique

Drawing, Cutting and Pasting

Materials

8 in. x 10 in. white paper
9 in. x 12 in. black paper
Colored markers
Scissors
Glue

Alternate Materials

Crayons; tempera paint; variety of markers such as scented, color overs, and stamp

Activities/Process

1. Read or give a summary of the book *Purple, Green and Yellow* by Robert Munsch, focusing on the illustrations.
2. On white paper with a black marker, trace the outline of your hand.
3. Design the hand with colored markers using lines, shapes, and patterns.
4. Cut the hand out, leaving about ¼ in. white edge of paper around the black line.
5. Glue the hand to the black paper.

Questions for Discussion

What kinds of lines did you use in your design? Point out some different shapes. Did you repeat anywhere? Do you have a favorite pattern of the ones you made?

Share Time/Evaluation

_____

_____

_____

_____

Curriculum Connection

Science, Social Studies, Math, Language Arts, Music

Curriculum Extensions

Science: Compare and contrast a variety of markers, such as permanent and washable. Learn about color dyes. Test washable and permanent markers on coffee filters by drawing with each then spraying the filter with a water bottle sprayer.

Social Studies: Learn about the art of Mehendi and the use of henna dye to decorate the human body. Talk about the use of tattoo in various cultures.

Math: Make various patterns and discuss the difference such as an AB pattern or an ABB pattern.

Language Arts: Make up your own story about what the girl might have done with the colored markers. Write a paragraph about you using markers. Make up a different ending to the story and tell what happened to the father after he left the house covered with markers.

Music: While listening to music, clap hands to the beat.

Hat Collage

Objectives/Concepts

1. To work with shape and color.
2. To experiment with drawing technique.
3. To experiment with cutting and pasting technique.
4. To work with collage.
5. To create texture.
6. To work with overlapping.

Technique

Drawing, Cutting and Pasting

Materials

12 in. x 18 in. white paper
Crayons
Colored paper scraps
Wallpaper
Tissue paper
Magazines
Gift wrapping paper
Scissors
Glue

Alternate Materials

Markers, chalk, tempera paint, buttons, yarn, pom-poms, feathers

Activities/Process

1. Read or give a summary of the book *Jennie's Hat* by Ezra Jack Keats, focusing on the illustrations.
2. On white paper with crayons, draw a large head, neck, and shoulders of a person.
3. Add facial features and hair.
4. Design the shoulders by making some kind of pattern for the clothing.
5. Design a hat for the portrait by the collage technique using the different paper varieties. Cut and glue some shapes and colors. Add some magazine or wrapping paper pictures.

Questions for Discussion

How did you make an oval shape from a rectangle? What is collage? What paper varieties did you use in the hat? Why did you choose the pictures you did from the magazine? How did you make the texture of the hair?

Share Time/Evaluation

_____

_____

_____

_____

Curriculum Connection

Social Studies, Language Arts, Physical Education

Curriculum Extensions

Social Studies: Look at different costumes and clothing worn around the world, specifically hats. Bring in different hats from community workers such as police officers, firefighters, nurses, construction workers, and others.

Language Arts: Read other books about hats. Make up your own story about a hat. Write a play in which the characters need to wear different hats.

Physical Education: Wear a hat and try to balance something on your head. Do relay games while balancing items on your head.

Hen

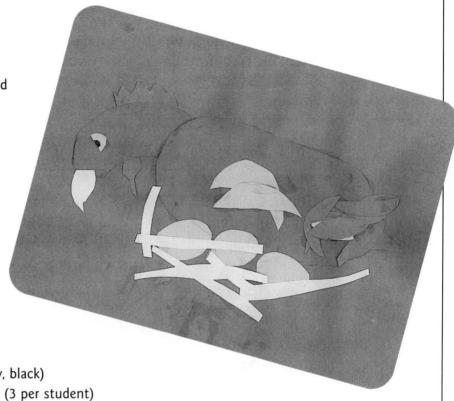

Objectives/Concepts

1. To work with shape and color.
2. To experiment with cutting and pasting technique.
3. To work with texture.

Technique

Cutting and Pasting

Materials

12 in. x 18 in. blue paper
6 in. x 9 in. brown paper
4½ in. x 6 in. brown paper
2 in. x 4½ in. brown paper
 (several pieces per student)
Colored paper scraps (red, yellow, black)
1½ in. x 2 in. tan or white paper (3 per student)
Feathers
Strips of yellow, tan, and light brown paper that were shredded in a paper shredder
Scissors
Glue

Alternate Materials

Tissue paper and other paper varieties, raffia, hay

Activities/Process

1. Read or give a summary of the book *Hattie and the Fox* by Mem Fox, focusing on the illustrations.
2. Round the edges of the 6 in. x 9 in. brown paper to make an oval for the hen's body.
3. Cut a neck and head from the 4½ in. x 6 in. brown paper and glue onto the body.
4. Round the edges of the 2 in. x 4½ in. brown paper to make feathers for the tail and wings. Glue down.
5. Glue down some craft feathers on top of the paper feathers.

6. Add beak, eyes, red comb, and other details to the hen.
7. Round the edges of the white or tan papers to make eggs.
8. Glue shredded paper to the blue paper to make a nest.
9. Glue the eggs in the nest and the hen on top of the nest.

Questions for Discussion

How did you make an oval shape from a rectangle? What shapes did you use to make the hen? How is texture shown in your picture?

Share Time/Evaluation

_____

_____

_____

_____

Curriculum Connection

Science, Social Studies, Math, Language Arts, Music, Physical Education

Curriculum Extensions

Science: Learn about different farm animals.

Social Studies: Visit a farm or have a farmer come into the classroom.

Math: Do different math equations using the number 12. A dozen hard-boiled eggs could be used.

Language Arts: Read other books about farm animals. Act out the story of Hattie and the fox. Put on a puppet show.

Music: Listen to and sing farm songs such as "Old MacDonald Had a Farm."

Physical Education: Play "The Farmer in the Dell." Play tag with someone pretending to be the fox.

Hot-Air
Henry

Hot Air Balloon

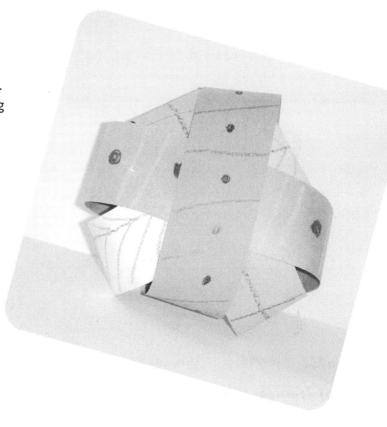

Objectives/Concepts

1. To work with line, shape, and color.
2. To experiment with drawing technique.
3. To experiment with cutting and pasting technique.
4. To experiment with sculpture.
5. To create with three-dimension.
6. To create pattern.
7. To make a mobile.

Technique

Drawing, Cutting and Pasting, Sculpture

Materials

1 in. x 12 in. light colored paper
   (4 per student)
Self-standing cupcake paper
Colored markers
Glue
Small piece of string or yarn

Alternate Materials

Crayons, colored paper, paper condiment container, small paper cup, papier-mâché, balloon

Activities/Process

1. Read or give a summary of the book *Hot-Air Henry* by Mary Calhoun, focusing on the illustrations.
2. On paper strips with colored markers, draw designs and patterns.
3. Glue one end of a strip to one side of the cupcake paper and the other end to the opposite side of the cupcake paper.
4. Glue the second strip halfway between the first strip in the same manner but also add a small drop of glue at the top to hold both strips together.

5. Glue the third and fourth strips between the first two, crossing over them and gluing them together at the top halfway point.
6. Attach the string or yarn to the top for hanging.

Questions for Discussion

What is a mobile? What is three-dimensional? What patterns did you make? Did you use different kind of lines and, if so, what kinds?

Share Time/Evaluation

_____

_____

_____

_____

Curriculum Connection

Science, Social Studies, Math, Language Arts, Music

Curriculum Extensions

Science: Learn about hot air balloons and do some experiments. Invite a hot air balloonist to the school to give a demonstration on the school grounds.

Social Studies: Chart on a map various hot air balloon flights.

Math: Make a variety of different patterns on different strips. Divide different size circles into eight sections. While doing science experiments, measure how high balloons rise.

Language Arts: Read other books about hot air balloons. Make up your own story about a ride in a hot air balloon.

Music: Listen to and sing songs about hot air balloons.

Jack-in-the-Box

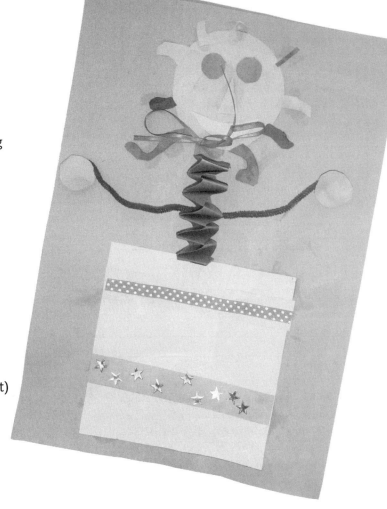

Objectives/Concepts

1. To work with line, shape, and color.
2. To create repetition.
3. To create pattern.
4. To create expression.
5. To experiment with cutting and pasting technique.
6. To create relief.

Technique

Cutting and Pasting

Materials

12 in. x 18 in. black paper
8 in. x 8 in. colored paper
5 in. x 5 in. skin-toned paper (a variety can be given to choose from)
1 in. x 18 in. colored strips (2 per student)
1 in. x 6 in. colored strips (2 of the same color per student)
Colored paper scraps
2 in. x 4 in. colored tissue paper
Scissors
Glue

Alternate Materials

Markers; crayons; tempera paint; watercolor paints; paper varieties; materials for three-dimensional project such as a small box, pipe cleaners, papier-mâché, yarn

Activities/Process

1. Read or give a summary of the book *Jack-in-the-Box* by Joy Cowley, focusing on the Jack-in-the-box toy.
2. Round the four corners of the skin-toned square to create a circle.
3. Glue the ends of the two long strips together perpendicularly to form a corner. Take the bottom strip and fold it over the top strip. Take the new bottom strip and fold it over the strip that just

became the top. Continue folding the bottom strip over the top strip until there is no more length of paper to fold. Put a dab of glue on the end to hold the strips together.

4. Glue one end of the folded strip to the circle, and the other end to the colored square.
5. Glue the circle and the square to the black paper so that the folded strip is in relief.
6. Glue the short strips to the folded strip and cut two similar shapes to glue on the ends for hands. The hands can be either glued to the paper or left to dangle.
7. Add hair and facial features with colored paper scraps.
8. Twist the tissue paper in the center to make a bow, and glue under the head for a tie.
9. With colored scraps, decorate the square box with lines and shapes to make patterns.

Questions for Discussion

How did you make a circle shape from a square? What is relief? How did you fold your paper to make it look like Jack could spring out of the box? What patterns did you create on the box? Why do you think toy inventors need to be creative?

Share Time/Evaluation

_____

_____

_____

_____

Curriculum Connection

Science, Social Studies, Math, Language Arts, Music, Physical Education

Curriculum Extensions

Science: Discuss inventions, force, movement, and tension. Make or draw an invention. Experiment with force using various strength springs.

Social Studies: Research toys found worldwide. Compare and contrast toys found in different areas of the world.

Math: Make different kinds of patterns using pattern blocks. Using a real Jack-in-the-box, estimate how many turns of the handle before Jack jumps out, then count as the handle is turned.

Language Arts: Pretend you are Jack-in-the-box and write a story or paragraph of an adventure when you jump out of the box. Write a rhyming poem about Jack-in-the-box.

Music: Listen to music that starts slow and builds tension, creating the feeling of winding something tight then releasing it.

Physical Education: While listening to music, pretend to be a Jack-in-the-box crouching down until the music changes and then jump up and shake around.

The Great Kapok Tree

Jungle or Rain Forest Scene

Objectives/Concepts

1. To work with line, shape, and color.
2. To blend and mix colors.
3. To create a variety of greens.
4. To work with overlapping.
5. To create texture.
6. To create density.
7. To experiment with drawing technique.
8. To experiment with cutting and pasting technique.

Technique

Drawing, Painting

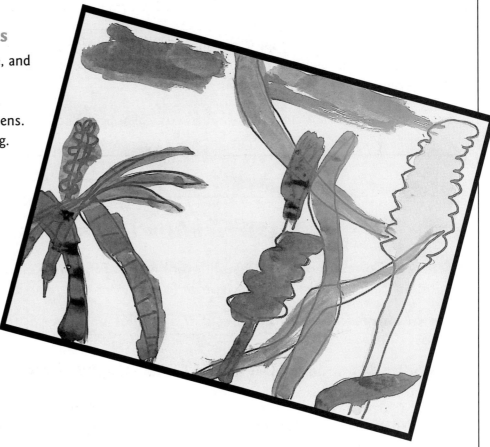

Materials

12 in. x 18 in. white paper
Black crayon
Watercolor paints

Alternate Materials

Crayons, markers, chalk, tempera paint, paper varieties

Activities/Process

1. Read or give a summary of the book *The Great Kapok Tree* by Lynne Cherry, focusing on the illustrations.
2. On white paper with black crayon, draw a jungle scene filling in the entire paper. Overlap to create a feeling of density.
3. Paint in with watercolor paints, mixing and blending colors to make a variety of greens.

Questions for Discussion

What might you find in a jungle or rain forest? What does *dense* mean and how can we create a feeling of density? How do we make the color green? How are the greens in your painting different? How did you show texture in your picture?

Share Time/Evaluation

_____

_____

_____

_____

Curriculum Connection

Science, Social Studies, Math, Language Arts, Music, Physical Education

Curriculum Extensions

Science: Compare and contrast different types of forests. Research the environment of a jungle or rain forest with the type of foliage, animals, and birds that exist in it.

Social Studies: Locate rain forests and jungles on a world map and learn about the areas.

Math: Using fruits that are found in the rain forest, cut them into sections for adding and subtracting. Make a chart of different fruits found in the rain forest.

Language Arts: Read other books about jungles or rain forests. Make up your own story about life in the rain forest. Be a news reporter and tell a story of your experience in the rain forest. Discover a new type of plant in a rain forest and write a description of it.

Music: Listen to music of the rain forest. Make instruments fashioned from rain forest instruments.

Physical Education: Be different animals of the rain forest and move around the room by crawling, jumping, flapping your arms, resting.

Ladybugs

Objectives/Concepts

1. To work with line, shape, color, and size.
2. To experiment with painting technique.
3. To create repetition.
4. To create pattern.
5. To experiment with color mixing.
6. To create overlapping.

Technique

Painting

Materials

12 in. x 18 in. white paper
Tempera paints (red, yellow, blue, and
    black)
Paint brushes

Alternate Materials

Markers, crayons, watercolor paints,
colored paper, tissue paper

Activities/Process

1. Read or give a summary of the book *The Grouchy Ladybug* by Eric Carle, focusing on the illustrations.
2. Paint several large ladybugs on the white paper. Vary the views with some side view, top view, or even upside down.
3. Around the ladybugs, paint overlapping leaves, mixing blue and yellow paint to make a variety of greens. Make it look like the ladybugs are resting or climbing on the leaves. Some leaves can be jaggered to look like the bugs have nibbled on them.
4. Blue paint can be used between the leaves to represent the sky.

Questions for Discussion

What shapes did you use to make the ladybugs? Where have you seen a ladybug? Are they always black and red? What two colors make green? How can you make a variety of the color green? Where did you overlap? Which leaf is in front of another leaf?

Share Time/Evaluation

_____

_____

_____

_____

Curriculum Connection

Science, Social Studies, Math, Language Arts, Music

Curriculum Extensions

Science: Look at different pictures of different kinds of ladybugs in insect books. Learn about insects. Look at ladybugs and other bugs under a magnifying glass.

Social Studies: Look up where ladybugs live and mark the locations on a map.

Math: Add and subtract using black circles on red paper.

Language Arts: Read other books about ladybugs. Make up your own story about a ladybug. Write a poem about a ladybug.

Music: Sing songs about ladybugs.

Merry-Go-Round Horse

Objectives/Concepts

1. To work with line, shape, and color.
2. To experiment with drawing technique.
3. To experiment with cutting and pasting technique.
4. To create texture.
5. To create three-dimension.
6. To create pattern.

Technique

Drawing, Cutting and Pasting, Sculpture

Materials

9 in. x 12 in. white scrap paper
9 in. x 12 in. colored paper (2 of the
    same color per student)
Colored paper scraps
Tissue paper
Glitter
Paper punch
Markers
Scissors
Glue
Plasticine clay
Wooden shish kebab skewer

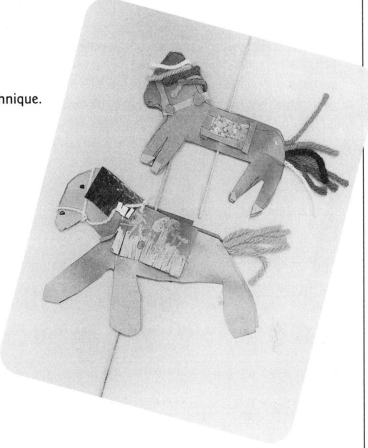

Alternate Materials

Tempera paint, pipe cleaners, feathers, yarn, paper punch, craft sticks or tongue depressors

Activities/Process

1. Read or give a summary of the book *Up and Down on the Merry-Go-Round* by Bill Martin, Jr. and John Archambault, focusing on the illustrations.
2. On white scrap paper, draw a horse, leaving off the mane and tail.
3. Cut out the horse, trace it on both pieces of the colored paper, and cut out those.
4. Lay the horses on the table so that they face each other before gluing the additions on. This way they will match up when gluing the two horse pieces together.

5. With a folded piece of paper or two papers of the same color held together, cut a blanket for the back of both horse shapes. Decorate with patterns, using markers, colored paper, glitter, or other materials. Glue in place.
6. Add eyes, nostrils, mouth, reins, and other details to both sides.
7. Cut one mane and tail. Glue to the back side of one horse shape.
8. Glue the wooden skewer to the back of one horse and glue both horse pieces together sandwiching in the skewer.
9. Stick the skewer into the ball of clay so that it will stand up.

Questions for Discussion

What shapes did you use to draw the horse? How did you make more than one of something? What patterns did you use? Does your horse look like it is running or jumping and why? How did you make something that was flat become three-dimensional?

Share Time/Evaluation

_____

_____

_____

_____

Curriculum Connection

Science, Social Studies, Math, Language Arts, Music, Physical Education

Curriculum Extensions

Science: Compare and contrast a variety of merry-go-rounds. Learn about movement, force, and energy.

Social Studies: Research where merry-go-rounds originated.

Math: Play a math game in which you stand or crouch according to whether the answer is odd or even.

Language Arts: Read other books about merry-go-rounds. Write a descriptive story about a merry-go-round. Write a poem about a merry-go-round.

Music: Listen to the type of music heard on a merry-go-round.

Physical Education: Do some activities that require up-and-down movement with bending and stretching.

Monster

Objectives/Concepts

1. To work with line, shape, and color.
2. To experiment with drawing technique.
3. To create pattern.

Technique

Drawing

Materials

12 in. x 18 in. white paper
Black marker
Crayons

Alternate Materials

Markers, chalk, tempera paint, watercolor
paint, colored paper

Activities/Process

1. Read or give a summary of the book
   The Monster at the End of This Book by Jon Stone,
   focusing on the illustrations.
2. On white paper with black marker, draw a large monster to fill the paper.
3. Add details and patterns with lines and shapes.
4. Color in with crayons.

Questions for Discussion

What shapes did you use to make your monster? Are monsters real? What does imagination mean?
Where did you use a pattern? Is your monster a scary or friendly monster? How can we tell?

Share Time/Evaluation

_____

_____

_____

_____

Curriculum Connection

Social Studies, Language Arts, Physical Education

Curriculum Extensions

Social Studies: Hear stories and view pictures about Greek mythical beasts.

Language Arts: Read books about monsters or mythical beasts. Using your imagination, write a descriptive paragraph describing a monster. Write a different ending to the story, having a different monster at the end of the book.

Physical Education: Play tag pretending to be monsters. Play hide-and-seek where those hiding pretend to be monsters.

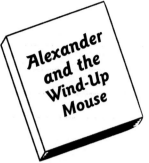

Mouse in Attic

Objectives/Concepts

1. To work with shape and color.
2. To experiment with cutting and pasting.
3. To experiment with collage.
4. To create texture.
5. To work with overlapping.

Technique

Cutting and Pasting

Materials

12 in. x 18 in. black paper
4½ in. x 6 in. dark gray paper
Colored paper scraps
Paper varieties (newspaper, magazine
    pages, wallpaper, paper bag, etc.)
Yarn, buttons, beads, material scraps
Scissors
Glue

Alternate Materials

Markers, chalk, tempera paint

Activities/Process

1. Read or give a summary of the book *Alexander and the Wind-Up Mouse* by Leo Lionni, focusing on the illustrations.
2. Tear an oval shape from the dark gray paper.
3. Cut and glue ears, legs, a tail, and an eye onto the gray oval to make a mouse.
4. Tear, cut, and crumble a variety of papers. Some can be made into actual objects such as bottles, vases, and toys.
5. Arrange torn and crumbled papers, objects, and the mouse by overlapping and glue onto the black paper.

Questions for Discussion

How did you make an oval shape from a rectangle? Why did you have to work very slowly when tearing the rectangular piece of paper into an oval shape? What does crumbling the paper do? What is texture? Where did you overlap?

Share Time/Evaluation

_____

_____

_____

_____

Curriculum Connection

Science, Social Studies, Math, Language Arts, Music, Physical Education

Curriculum Extensions

Science: Do some research on mice. Have a mouse as a class pet.

Social Studies: Learn about different toys from different parts of the world.

Math: Make a hidden picture drawing by hiding several mice in the drawing. Swap pictures and find each other's mice.

Language Arts: Read other books about mice. Make up another story about Alexander the Mouse. Tell a story about what you might find in an attic.

Music: Sing songs and do finger plays about mice.

Physical Education: Play cat and mouse tag. Pretend that you are a wind-up mouse and have someone wind you up. Move around the room until you need to be wound up again.

No Dodos

Panda Bear

Objectives/Concepts

1. To work with shape and color.
2. To experiment with painting technique.

Technique

Painting

Materials

12 in. x 18 in. red paper
Tempera paints (black and white)

Alternate Materials

Markers, crayons, colored paper

Activities/Process

1. Read or give a summary of the book
   No Dodos by Amanda Wallwork,
   focusing on the illustrations.
2. On red paper with white paint, paint a large circle for
   the panda's head and a larger oval for the body.
3. Paint black arms and legs.
4. Paint over the top of the white oval with black as if the panda was wearing a jacket.
5. Paint two black ears, large black eyes, and a black nose and mouth.

Questions for Discussion

What shapes did you use to make the panda? What does *endangered* mean? What is *extinct*? What
happened if the white paint was not dry before you painted black over it?

_____

_____

_____

_____

Curriculum Connection

Science, Social Studies, Math, Language Arts, Music, Physical Education

Curriculum Extensions

Science: Research panda bears and compare to other kinds of bears. Research other endangered animals, where they live, and what can be done to help them survive.

Social Studies: Locate China on a map and learn a little about the country that panda bears come from. Locate where other endangered animals live and locate those areas on the map.

Math: Count along with the book *No Dodos*. Gather things around the room and bring them to an area where you can count one of something, two of something else, and so on. Play other counting games.

Language Arts: Read other counting books. Write your own counting book. Make up your own story about a panda bear. Write a paragraph on what can be done to help protect endangered animals.

Music: Listen to and sing counting songs.

Physical Education: Have some students pretend to be endangered animals and have the rest of the group look for them in a hide-and-seek game.

Parrot

Objectives/Concepts

1. To work with line, shape, and color.
2. To experiment with drawing technique.

Technique

Drawing

Materials

12 in. x 18 in. white paper
Oil crayons

Alternate Materials

Markers, chalk, tempera paint, watercolor
paint, colored papers

Activities/Process

1. Read or give a summary of the book
   Papagayo by Gerald McDermott,
   focusing on the illustrations.
2. On white paper with crayons, draw the shapes to make a
   large parrot.
3. Fill the shapes with straight and zigzag lines.
4. Color in between lines to make straight and zigzag stripes.

Questions for Discussion

What shapes did you use to make the bird? Did you blend any colors together? What kinds of animals
might come out at night?

_____

_____

_____

_____

Curriculum Connection

Science, Social Studies, Math, Language Arts, Music, Physical Education

Curriculum Extensions

Science: Find out some information about parrots. Have a person from a pet store bring in a parrot. Discuss animals that are nocturnal. Learn about a rain forest environment. Make a model to show the phases of the moon.

Social Studies: On a map, locate the Amazon rain forest. Read about and locate other rain forests.

Math: Chart the phases of the moon. Keep track for a month.

Language Arts: Read other books about parrots, the rain forest and the moon. Write a story about a mischief maker. Make puppets and put on a play about the book *Papagayo*.

Music: Listen to the music of the rain forest. Sing rain forest songs.

Physical Education: Play chase games with one person acting as the moon-dog tagging other students. When students get tagged, they will freeze until the parrot, another student, tags them.

Patriotic Parade

Objectives/Concepts

1. To work with line, shape, and color.
2. To experiment with drawing technique.
3. To experiment with printing technique.
4. To experiment with cutting and pasting technique.
5. To work with the human form in figure drawing.
6. To work with silhouette.

Technique

Drawing, Printing, Cutting and Pasting

Materials

12 in. x 18 in. blue paper
8 in. x 14 in. red paper
½ in. x 14 in. white paper (6 per student)
6 in. x 8 in. blue paper
Scissors
Glue
1½ in. star-shaped sponge
White tempera paint

Alternate Materials

Markers, chalk, crayons, colored paper varieties

Activities/Process

1. Read or give a summary of the book *Parade* by Donald Crews, focusing on the illustrations.
2. Glue the white strips to the red paper evenly spaced.

3. Glue the red and white striped paper to the blue paper, leaving a 2 in. border on all sides.
4. Draw the outline of a human form on the smaller blue paper. The arms should be positioned to hold a flag, and the legs should be drawn as if marching.
5. Cut the silhouette out and glue over the striped paper.
6. Glue an American flag in the hand of the body. (Packages of small pre-made flags on toothpicks can be purchased at party goods stores or flags can be handmade in class.)
7. Using white paint, print stars around the edges of the large blue paper to make a border.

Questions for Discussion

What is a parade? What are some occasions to have a parade? What does it mean to be patriotic? What is a silhouette? How did you position the body to make it look like it was walking or marching? What is printing? What happened if you had too much paint on your sponge? What happened if you did not have enough paint?

Share Time/Evaluation

_____

_____

_____

_____

Curriculum Connection

Science, Social Studies, Math, Language Arts, Music, Physical Education

Curriculum Extensions

Science: View a model of the human skeleton.

Social Studies: Research different types of parades held in different countries. Make flags of different nations.

Math: Make a variety of stripes spaced evenly on different size papers. Create different patterns.

Language Arts: Read books about parades and patriotic celebrations. Write a story about a parade. Describe a parade in a paragraph. Write a poem about a parade.

Music: Sing patriotic songs. Play or listen to instruments seen in a parade.

Physical Education: March around the gym or the school.

Printed Fish

Objectives/Concepts

1. To work with shape, and color.
2. To experiment with printing technique.
3. To experiment with roller painting technique.
4. To experiment with cutting and pasting technique.
5. To use repetition.
6. To create overlapping.

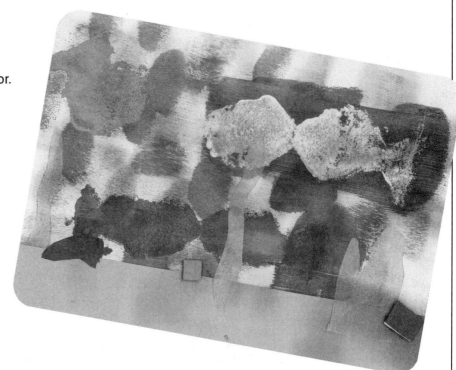

Technique

Painting, Printing, Cutting and Pasting

Materials

12 in. x 18 in. white paper
2 in. x 18 in. light brown paper
Sponge roller
Tempera paint (blue, red, yellow, orange)
Sponge cut in the shape of a fish
Scissors
Glue
Colored paper scraps

Alternate Materials

Markers, chalk, crayons, watercolor paints

Activities/Process

1. Read or give a summary of the book *Swimmy* by Leo Lionni, focusing on the illustrations.
2. With the sponge roller, roll blue paint onto the white paper creating the texture of water.

3. Glue the light brown paper to the bottom edge creating the sand.
4. Sponge print several fish shapes with yellow, red, and orange paint on top of the blue paint.
5. Cut and glue weeds, rocks, shells and other underwater life from colored scraps, making sure to overlap some.

Questions for Discussion

Why might fish swim in groups? What makes the blue roller painted area look like water? How do the fish prints look alike? How do they look different? Where is there overlapping in the art work? What happened if you used too much paint? What happened if you did not use enough paint?

Share Time/Evaluation

_____

_____

_____

_____

Curriculum Connection

Science, Math, Language Arts, Music, Physical Education

Curriculum Extensions

Science: Compare and contrast a variety of fish by noticing the color, shape, and size of each. Keep an aquarium in the classroom.

Math: Make a graph of different kinds of aquarium fish and their sizes. Estimate how many fish-shaped crackers are in a bag. Do some adding and subtracting using fish-shaped crackers.

Language Arts: Read other books about fish. Make up your own story about the adventures of a fish. Write a paragraph about what can be accomplished in a group that cannot be accomplished by oneself.

Music: Sing songs about fish.

Physical Education: Move around as if you were a fish.

Raven

Objectives/Concepts

1. To work with line, shape, and color.
2. To create patterns.
3. To work with layering.
4. To experiment with painting technique.
5. To experiment with cutting and pasting technique.

Technique

Painting, Cutting and Pasting

Materials

12 in. x 12 in. black paper
8 in. x 8 in. white paper
4½ in. x 6 in. black paper
3 in. x 4½ in. black paper (3 per student)
3 in. x 3 in. black paper

Colored paper scraps
Watercolor paints
Scissors
Glue

Alternate Materials

Markers, chalk, tempera paint

Activities/Process

1. Read or give a summary of the book *Raven* by Gerald McDermott, focusing on the illustrations.
2. On white paper, paint a sky blending either daytime colors (blue, green, or purple) or sunset colors (yellow, red, or orange).
3. Cut an oval shape from the 4½ x 6 in. black paper for the bird's body.
4. Cut a long triangle from the 3 in. x 4½ in. black paper for the tail.
5. Cut two half ovals from the other 3 in. x 4½ in. black paper for the wings.

6. Cut a circle from the 3 in. square for the head of the bird.
7. Using black scraps, cut a long beak.
8. Glue the pieces together to make the shape of the bird and glue on the painted paper.
9. Glue to the 12 in. square black paper.
10. With colored scraps, make the eye.
11. Cut a variety of shapes and glue onto the bird's body, wings, and tail.
12. Cut a variety of shapes and glue down layering some on top of each other around the black border to make patterns.

Questions for Discussion

What shapes did you use to make the bird? What patterns did you make? How did you make more than one of the same shapes? Where did you layer colors and shapes? How did you blend colors in your sky? What makes it look like the bird is flying? What is a myth?

Share Time/Evaluation

_____

_____

_____

_____

Curriculum Connection

Science, Social Studies, Math, Language Arts, Music, Physical Education

Curriculum Extensions

Science: Do some research on the raven. Hang some string or yarn from tree branches and add something shiny such as silver or gold ribbon.

Social Studies: Research the Pacific Northwest. Color in the area on a map. Find more information on Pacific Northwest Native Americans.

Math: Create paper strips with patterns on them. Change patterns on each strip.

Language Arts: Read other books about Pacific Northwest Native Americans. Make up your own myth about a raven.

Music: Listen to Pacific Northwest Native American music. Keep the beat of the music with different instruments such as drums.

Physical Education: Pretend that you are a bird and move carefully around the room. Try gliding, flapping, and landing.

Too
Many
Books

Reading a Book

Objectives/Concepts

1. To work with line, shape, and color.
2. To experiment with drawing technique.
3. To experiment with cutting and pasting technique.
4. To create texture.
5. To create relief.

Technique

Drawing, Cutting and Pasting

Materials

12 in. x 18 in. colored paper
9 in. x 12 in. paper in a variety of skin tones
4½ in. x 6 in. paper in a variety of skin tones
6 in. x 9 in. paper in a variety of skin tones
4 in. x 12 in. colored paper
8 in. x 11 in. colored paper
Colored paper scraps
Crayons
Scissors
Glue

Alternate Materials

Markers, yarn, paper varieties

Activities/Process

1. Read or give a summary of the book *Too Many Books* by Caroline Feller Bauer, focusing on the illustrations.
2. Fold the 8 in. x 11 in. colored paper in half and with crayons draw and label a book cover of a favorite book.

3. Round the corners of the 9 in. x 12 in. skin-toned paper.

4. Glue the oval to the top of the large colored paper leaving enough room for hair or a hat.

5. Glue the 4½ in. x 6 in. paper to the bottom of the oval.

6. Round the top corners of the 4 in. x 12 in. paper and glue below the neck for the shoulders.

7. With colored scraps, add facial features, hair, eyeglasses, or other details.

8. Trace both hands on the 6 in. x 9 in. skin-toned paper, cut out, and glue to the book cover.

9. At the bottom of the paper, glue the side edges of the book so that it comes away from the face in relief.

Questions for Discussion

How did you make an oval shape from a rectangle? Which way did you have to glue the hands so that it looks like the person is holding the book? What does relief mean? How did you make the texture of the hair? Which book did you choose to illustrate the cover for?

Share Time/Evaluation

_____

_____

_____

_____

Curriculum Connection

Science, Social Studies, Math, Language Arts, Music

Curriculum Extensions

Science: Discuss facial features and the proportion of one to another. Look at a model of a human skull.

Social Studies: Note multicultural differences of people from various geographical areas. Research different ways to record stories other than books, such as scrolls or clay tablets.

Math: Make equations using the numbers from book pages by closing and opening a book randomly. Chart different types of books checked out of the library after a class visit.

Language Arts: Read different types of books. Write your own book. Write a story about the person reading the book. Write a summary of the book the person is reading.

Music: Look at music books and learn to identify some musical notes and symbols.

The Screaming Mean Machine

Roller Coaster

Objectives/Concepts

1. To work with line variety.
2. To experiment with abstract.
3. To create three-dimension.
4. To work with layering.
5. To work with overlapping.
6. To experiment with folding, curling, and interlocking.
7. To create patterns.
8. To experiment with sculpture.
9. To experiment with cutting and pasting technique.

Technique

Cutting and Pasting, Sculpture

Materials

9 in. x 12 in. black paper
Colored paper strips (variety of lengths and thickness)
Paper punch
Scissors
Glue

Alternate Materials

Markers, paper varieties, stick-on stars or other shapes, glitter, fancy-edged scissors

Activities/Process

1. Read or give a summary of the book *The Screaming Mean Machine* by Joy Cowley, focusing on the illustrations.
2. Discuss architecture as a form of art.
3. Glue one end of a colored strip to the 9 in. x 12 in. black paper.

4. Bend, fold, or curve the strip before gluing the other end to the black paper.
5. Continue gluing strips to the black paper in a variety of ways. Holes can be punched out of some strips, or some punched circles can be added to other strips to create a pattern. Strips can be cut thinner and glued on top of other strips before gluing to the black paper. Stripes can be added for patterns. Zigzag, wavy, or curved edges can be cut from the strips. Strips can go over or under each other in an interlocking or intertwining fashion.

Questions for Discussion

What is a roller coaster? What is architecture? What is three-dimensional? Have you ever been on or seen a roller coaster? How did you feel while riding it or watching it? What made you feel that way? Was there a tunnel on the ride? What form is a tunnel? How did you use the strips to create the turning effect of the roller coaster? How did you change some of the strips? Did you use a pattern anywhere? Tell me about your roller coaster.

Share Time/Evaluation

_____

_____

_____

_____

Curriculum Connection

Science, Social Studies, Math, Language Arts, Music, Physical Education

Curriculum Extensions

Science: Compare and contrast a variety of roller coasters. Learn about force, friction, and motion.

Social Studies: Locate where major roller coaster rides are located.

Math: Work with shapes and forms.

Language Arts: Read other books about roller coasters. Make up your own story about a ride on a roller coaster. Write a poem about the feelings experienced on a roller coaster ride. Describe a screaming mean machine.

Music: Listen to amusement park music.

Physical Education: Go to a creative playground. Do some tumbling and turning games.

School Bus

Objectives/Concepts

1. To work with line, shape, and color.
2. To experiment with drawing technique.
3. To create texture.
4. To work with pattern.

Technique

Drawing

Materials

12 in. x 18 in. white paper
Black marker
Crayons

Alternate Materials

Watercolor paint, tempera paint, colored paper

Activities/Process

1. Read or give a summary of the book *School Bus* by Donald Crews, focusing on the illustrations.
2. On white paper with black marker, draw a bus. This can be accomplished with a long rectangle for the body of the bus, and then adding a shorter rectangle with rounded off corners to the top leaving the front of the bus coming further out.
3. Add circles for wheels.
4. Divide the top part into four squares or rectangles by drawing vertical lines.
5. Inside the squares or rectangles, draw circles for heads and curved shoulders.
6. Add details of hair, faces, and clothing patterns and designs.
7. Draw the details of the bus by making the door, headlights, tailpipe, and so on.
8. Add the road and lines for landscape details.
9. Color in with crayons.

Questions for Discussion

What shapes did you use to make the bus? What details did you draw on the bus? What makes the children riding in the bus look different? What kinds of lines did you use to show the texture of the hair? What patterns did you use in the clothing? What is a picture book?

Share Time/Evaluation

_____

_____

_____

_____

Curriculum Connection

Science, Social Studies, Math, Language Arts, Music

Curriculum Extensions

Science: Compare and contrast physical features of people.

Social Studies: Discuss the multicultural aspects of children around the world. Research different types of transportation. Go on a bus ride and learn about bus safety.

Math: Make a graph about how many children in the class ride which buses to and from school. Do math equations varying the amount of children and the number of seats on a bus.

Language Arts: Read other books about buses and other modes of transportation. Make up your own story about riding a bus. Make up a story about someone you met on a bus. Write a letter to someone who rides on your bus, or if you walk to school, you can write it to someone you know who rides the bus.

Music: Sing verses to a song about the children on the bus.

Of Lucky Pebbles and Mermaid's Tears

Sea Glass and Shells in a Bottle

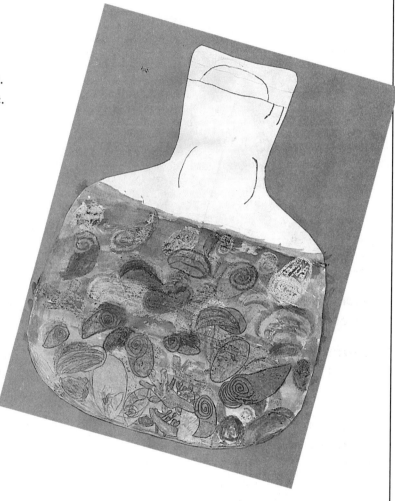

Objectives/Concepts

1. To work with line, shape, and color.
2. To experiment with drawing technique.
3. To experiment with painting technique.
4. To work with overlapping.
5. To create texture.
6. To create a three-dimensional effect.

Technique

Drawing, Painting, Cutting and Pasting

Materials

12 in. x 18 in. colored paper
12 in. x 18 in. white paper
Pencils
Watercolor paints
Scissors
Glue

Alternate Materials

Chalk, colored pencils

Activities/Process

1. Read or give a summary of the book *Of Lucky Pebbles and Mermaid's Tears* by Mimi Gregoire Carpenter, focusing on the illustrations.
2. Fold white paper in half; on the outside edge draw half the shape of a bottle. Cut on the line and unfold.
3. Observe sea glass, shells, rocks, and other small findings along the sea's edge.
4. With pencil, draw the outline of little pieces of sea glass, pebbles, rocks, and shells on the bottle-shaped paper, overlapping them.
5. Paint in with watercolor paints.

6. With either pencil or paint, make some shadow areas on the edges of the bottle.

7. Glue the bottle to the colored paper.

Questions for Discussion

How does sea glass feel? What makes it that way? How did you show the texture of the shells? What happened when you painted colors next to each other and they were still wet? Did you mix any colors? What happened? How did you show light and dark in your paints? Why did you have to overlap? What did you do to make the bottle seem three-dimensional?

Share Time/Evaluation

_____

_____

_____

_____

Curriculum Connection

Science, Social Studies, Math, Language Arts, Music, Physical Education

Curriculum Extensions

Science: Compare and contrast a variety of shells, sea glass, and other findings from the ocean edge by noticing the color, shape, and size of each. Discuss the environment of the ocean and the need to clean up waste and recycle. Visit a recycling bottle plant.

Social Studies: Locate the oceans on a map and research the areas.

Math: Make math equations using pebbles, small shells, and sea glass. Estimate how many pieces of sea glass, pebbles, and shells are in a bottle and then count them. Collect bottles, redeem them, and spend the money on something for the environment.

Language Arts: Read other books about oceans, shells, and the sea environment. Make up your own story about a sea creature. Make a wish on a piece of sea glass and write about it. Make posters on recycling.

Music: Listen to and sing songs about the sea.

Physical Education: Move your body as if you were a pebble in the ocean, swaying back and forth and being turned around.

Skeletons

Objectives/Concepts

1. To work with line and shape.
2. To experiment with drawing technique.
3. To experiment with cutting and pasting technique.
4. To create movement.
5. To work with proportion.
6. To create facial expression.

Technique

Drawing, Cutting and Pasting

Materials

12 in. x 18 in. black paper
12 in. x 18 in. white paper
1½ in. x 2 in. oak tag (2 per student)
2 in. x 2 in. oak tag
1 in. x 2½ in. oak tag (2 per student)
1 in. x 2 in. oak tag

1 in. x 1 in. oak tag
  (2 per student)
Pencil
Scissors
Glue
Fine-line black marker

Alternate Materials

White chalk, white tempera paint, white charcoal pencil

Activities/Process

1. Read or give a summary of the book *Funnybones* by Janet and Allan Ahlberg, focusing on the illustrations.
2. Round corners of 2 in. x 2 in. oak tag paper for chest.
3. On one of the 1½ in. x 2 in. oak tag with pencil, draw an upside down pear shape and cut it out for the head.
4. On the other 1½ in. x 2 in. paper, draw the number 8 having it touch the edges of the oak tag for the pelvic area. Cut it out.
5. On one piece of 1 in. x 2½ in. oak tag for the legs, draw the shape of a bone so that the two edges of each look like the top of a heart. Cut it out.
6. On the other 1 in. x 2½ in. paper draw a slightly smaller size bone for the arms. Cut it out.
7. Make the 1 in. x 2 in. paper into a bone shape for the feet.

8. On one piece of the 1 in. x 1 in. paper draw a hand and cut it out.
9. On the other 1 in. x 1 in. piece of oak tag, draw a small rectangle with curvy edges for the neck and spine.
10. Trace the oak tag shapes onto white paper and cut out. Make sure two hands and two feet are cut as well as four parts for the arms and legs.
11. Arrange the skeleton and glue it down on the black paper. If time allows, use the oak tag to make more bodies and glue onto the same black paper.
12. These directions are for advanced skills, but this lesson can be easily adapted to moderate by making oval shapes instead of the actual shape of the bones. To make the lesson even easier, larger pieces can be used from white paper and cut out directly, eliminating the need to trace the shapes from the oak tag to the white paper.
13. With the fine-line black marker draw the lines for the ribs and spine as well as give the skeleton some kind of facial expression.

Questions for Discussion

How did you make some of your shapes? What is bigger—our arms or our legs? What does the expression on your skeleton look like? How did you show the texture of the ribs? Can you put your body in the same position as the skeleton you made?

Share Time/Evaluation

_____

_____

_____

_____

Curriculum Connection

Science, Math, Language Arts, Music, Physical Education

Curriculum Extensions

Science: Look at a model of the human skeleton. Learn about different bones. Invite a nurse into the classroom to discuss bone structure and how to stay healthy.

Math: Estimate how many bones are in the human body and then look it up. Estimate how many dog bone treats are in a jar, then donate them to the animal society. Measure how tall each other is.

Language Arts: Read other books about the human body or skeletons. Make up your own story about a skeleton. Write a paragraph describing the bones in the human body.

Music: Listen to and sing the song about bones being connected to different bones.

Physical Education: Do different exercises and notice the position the body is in. Play "Simon Says" by touching different bones in the body.

Snail Design

Objectives/Concepts

1. To work with line, shape, and color.
2. To experiment with drawing technique.
3. To experiment with painting technique.
4. To use horizontal and vertical lines.
5. To create spiral lines.
6. To create a pattern through repetition.

Technique

Drawing, Painting

Materials

12 in. x 18 in. white paper
Permanent black marker
Watercolor paints

Alternate Materials

Crayons (wax or oil), markers, chalk, tempera paint, gadgets for stamp printing

Activities/Process

1. Read or give a summary of the book *The Biggest House in the World* by Leo Lionni, focusing on the illustrations.
2. On 12 in. x 18 in. white paper with a permanent black marker, draw a large spiral in the middle of the paper to represent the shell of a snail.
3. Add the outline of a body, head, antennae, and facial features to the snail shell.
4. Using different lines and shapes, draw patterns in the snail's shell.
5. All around the snail draw different size spirals.

6. Add repeated short horizontal and vertical lines around the spirals.

7. Paint the snail and the spirals with watercolor paints.

Questions for Discussion

How did you make a spiral? What shapes did you use to make the snail? What happened when you painted colors next to each other and they were still wet? Did you make any colors from mixing other colors together? What colors did you use and what colors did they make? Where did you use patterns and what kind of patterns are they?

Share Time/Evaluation

_____

_____

_____

_____

Curriculum Connection

Science, Social Studies, Math, Language Arts, Physical Education

Curriculum Extensions

Science: Compare and contrast different kinds of snails, what they eat, and where they live. In a container, make an environment for snails in the classroom and watch how they eat. Find or list other things in nature that have a spiral design.

Social Studies: Discuss different types of houses for animals and people.

Math: Measure and weigh different shells. Make different patterns using toothpicks as the horizontal and vertical lines.

Language Arts: Read other books about snails. Make up your own story about a snail. Tell a story about how your house might change. Have you ever done anything that you thought might be good but worked out otherwise? Write about what you learned from that experience.

Physical Education: Pretend that you are a snail and slowly crawl around the room. Crawl as if you have a light shell and then as if you have a large heavy shell.

The Biggest House in the World

Snail in an Environment

Objectives/Concepts

1. To work with line, shape, and color.
2. To experiment with drawing technique.
3. To experiment with tearing and pasting technique.
4. To experiment with paper mosaic.
5. To create an environment for a snail.
6. To create texture.
7. To create a focal point or emphasis.

Technique

Drawing, Painting, Cutting (Tearing) and Pasting

Materials

12 in. x 18 in. white paper
Black marker
Crayons (wax or oil)
Colored paper scraps
Glue

Alternate Materials

Colored markers, colored pencils, paper punch, paper varieties

Activities/Process

1. Read or give a summary of the book *The Biggest House in the World* by Leo Lionni, focusing on the illustrations.
2. On 12 in. x 18 in. white paper with a black marker, draw a large spiral in the middle of the paper to represent the shell of a snail.

3. Add the outline of a body, head, antennae, and facial features to the snail shell.
4. Draw an environment for the snail.
5. Color in everything but the snail's shell.
6. Tear small pieces of colored paper and glue onto the snail's shell.

Questions for Discussion

How did you make a spiral? What shapes did you use to make the snail? What type of environment did you make for the snail? What is mosaic? What part of the artwork do we notice first and why?

Share Time/Evaluation

_____

_____

_____

_____

Curriculum Connection

Science, Social Studies, Math, Language Arts, Physical Education

Curriculum Extensions

Science: Compare and contrast different kinds of snails, what they eat, and where they live. In a container, make an environment for snails in the classroom and watch how they eat. Find or list other things in nature that have a spiral design.

Social Studies: Discuss different types of houses for animals and people.

Math: Measure and weigh different shells.

Language Arts: Read other books about snails. Make up your own story about a snail. Tell a story about how your house might change. Have you ever done anything that you thought might be good but worked out otherwise? Write about what you learned from that experience.

Physical Education: Pretend you are a snail and slowly crawl around the room. Crawl as if you have a light shell and then as if you have a large heavy shell.

Snake

Objectives/Concepts

1. To work with line, shape, and color.
2. To experiment with painting technique.
3. To create pattern.

Technique

Painting

Materials

12 in. x 18 in. black paper
Tempera paints

Alternate Materials

Markers, crayons, chalk, watercolor paints, colored papers

Activities/Process

1. Read or give a summary of the book *Hide and Snake* by Keith Baker, focusing on the illustrations.
2. On black paper outline a snake with paint so that the body curls or coils.
3. Paint lines, shapes, and colors to make a patterned body.
4. Paint eyes, nostrils, mouth, and tongue.

Questions for Discussion

How did you make the lines of the snake curve or coil? What pattern did you create? What happened when you painted colors next to each other and they were still wet? Did you make any colors by mixing other colors together?

_____

_____

_____

_____

Curriculum Connection

Science, Social Studies, Math, Language Arts, Physical Education

Curriculum Extensions

Science: Compare and contrast a variety of snakes by noticing the color, shape, and size of each. Take a field trip to a pet store that has snakes or invite a speaker into the classroom.

Social Studies: Learn where snakes live and compare those parts of the world to the kinds of snakes that inhabit the area.

Math: Make a variety of patterns.

Language Arts: Read other books about snakes. Make up your own story about an apple.

Physical Education: Play hide-and-snake (seek).

Snowman

Objectives/Concepts

1. To work with line, shape, and color.
2. To experiment with drawing technique.
3. To experiment with printing technique.
4. To experiment with cutting and pasting technique.
5. To create texture.
6. To experiment with color blending.
7. To work with silhouette.
8. To create distance.

Technique

Drawing, Printing, Cutting and Pasting

Materials

12 in. x 18 in. blue paper
Black crayon
Colored chalk
White tempera paint
1 in. sponge piece
Colored paper scraps
Scissors
Glue

Alternate Materials

Buttons, yarn, material scraps, paper varieties, cotton balls

Activities/Process

1. Read or give a summary of the book *The Snowman* by Raymond Briggs, focusing on the illustrations.

2. On the top third of the blue paper, blend colored chalk to make a sky.
3. With black crayon, draw the outline of a large snowman. Add silhouette mountains, trees, houses, or other landscape images.
4. Sponge print the snowman with white paint.
5. Add some printed snow on the ground.
6. With colored paper, cut and glue facial features, clothing, and other details to the snowman.

Questions for Discussion

What shapes did you use for your snowman? What is silhouette? What colors did you use in your sky? Were other colors made from blending them together? How is distance shown in your picture? How did you create the texture of snow?

Share Time/Evaluation

_____

_____

_____

_____

Curriculum Connection

Science, Social Studies, Math, Language Arts, Physical Education

Curriculum Extensions

Science: Discuss why it snows. Invite a meteorologist to visit the classroom.

Social Studies: Color in places on a world map where it might snow.

Math: Add and subtract using marshmallows as snowballs.

Language Arts: Read other books about snow. Make up your own story about a snowstorm. Create a snowman character and introduce him to the class. Tell a story about him. Read and write poems about snow.

Physical Education: Crumple up white scrap paper from the recycle bin into balls. Use them to have a snowball fight or play games with them in the gym. Weather permitting, go outside and build snow characters.

Spider

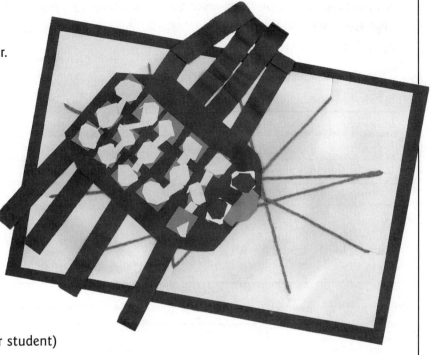

Objectives/Concepts

1. To work with line, shape, and color.
2. To create patterns.
3. To work with layering.
4. To work with folding.
5. To experiment with cutting and pasting technique.

Technique

Cutting and Pasting

Materials

12 in. x 18 in. colored paper
9 in. x 12 in. black paper
¼ in. x 6 in. black paper strips (8 per student)
Assorted colored paper scraps
Scissors
Glue
Yarn or string

Alternate Materials

Markers, crayons (wax or oil), chalk, tempera paint, glitter, paper punch

Activities/Process

1. Read or give a summary of the book *The Very Busy Spider* by Eric Carle, focusing on the illustrations.
2. On all the edges of the 12 in. x 18 in. colored paper, cut 4 or 5 small slits.
3. With yarn or string, start on the back of the paper and pull the string to the front, through one slit. Cross the yarn or string over the top of the paper and go through a different slit to the back. Bring the yarn or string back to the front through a neighboring slit. Continue this process making the spider's web. Tape the two ends of yarn or string on the back side.
4. Round the edges of the 9 in. x 12 in. black paper to make an oval for the spider's body.
5. Add facial features to the spider.

6. Create patterns with colored shapes for the spider's back. Layer colors and shapes on top of each other.
7. Fold the black strips back and forth with about ½ in. folds and glue to the body for the legs.
8. Glue the spider to the web.

Questions for Discussion

How did you make an oval shape from a rectangle? What shapes did you use to make patterns on the spider's back? Where did you layer colors and shapes? Why do spiders spin webs? How do the lines you made with yarn or string resemble a spider's web? What happened to the legs when you folded the paper back and forth?

Share Time/Evaluation

_____
_____
_____
_____

Curriculum Connection

Science, Math, Language Arts, Music

Curriculum Extensions

Science: Compare and contrast a variety of spiders by noticing the color, shape, and size of each. Look for spider webs and notice the lines and design of the web.

Math: Create different pattern formations using geometric shapes. Add, subtract, multiply, or divide using the number 8.

Language Arts: Read other books about spiders. Act out nursery rhymes about spiders. Tell a spooky story about a spider.

Music: Sing spider songs.

Why the Sun and Moon Live in the Sky

Sun and Moon Mobile

Objectives/Concepts

1. To work with line, shape, and color.
2. To experiment with cutting and pasting.
3. To experiment with mobiles.
4. To work with three-dimension.
5. To create balance.

Technique

Cutting and Pasting, Sculpture

Materials

4 in. x 4 in. yellow or orange paper
  (2 of the same color per student)
4 in. x 4 in. white paper
Colored paper scraps
Scissors
Glue
Wooden shish kebab stick
String or yarn
Paper punch

Alternate Materials

Markers, tissue paper, pipe cleaner, craft stick,
clothes hanger or other hanging device

Activities/Process

1. Read or give a summary of the book *Why the Sun and the Moon Live in the Sky* by Elphinstone Dayrell, focusing on the illustrations.
2. Round the corners of both the yellow or orange papers to make a circle for a sun.
3. With the other color, cut triangles, ovals, rectangles, or some other shape to make sunrays. These can be alternated, or additional warm colors can be used to make a pattern.
4. Glue shapes around the back edges of one circle.
5. With colored scraps, cut facial features and shapes for design. Cut enough to have both circles the same. Glue the details on the circles, then glue the two circles together so that the sun rays are in between.

6. Using white paper, cut a shape for the moon. This can be any part of a circle such as a quarter, half, crescent, or a full circle.
7. With colored scraps, make the facial features and designs for the moon face, remembering to make two of everything in order to decorate both sides of the moon shape.
8. Tie one end of a string or piece of yarn to the middle of the skewer.
9. Punch a hole in the top of both the sun and moon and tie a similar length string to each.
10. Tie the other ends of the yarn or string to the stick. The lengths might need to be adjusted depending on the weight of the sun and moon in order to make it balance. Younger children will need help putting the mobile together.

Questions for Discussion

What is a mobile? What shapes did you use in your sun and moon? What are warm colors? How did you get the same thing on both sides of your sun and moon? What is balance? How did you get your mobile to balance? What is a folktale?

Share Time/Evaluation

_____

_____

_____

_____

Curriculum Connection

Science, Social Studies, Math, Language Arts, Music, Physical Education

Curriculum Extensions

Science: Research and learn about the sun, moon, ocean, and the animals that live in the water. Learn about movement and balance.

Social Studies: Locate Africa on a map. Find where Nigeria is located. Learn more about African tribes.

Math: Work with shapes and patterns. Experiment with balance.

Language Arts: Read or listen to other folktales. Invite a storyteller in or take a trip to the library to hear some stories. Make up your own folktale.

Music: Listen to African music.

Physical Education: Learn African dances. Try to balance different classmates on a see-saw. Walk on a balance beam. Try different arm positions while trying to balance on one foot.

Sun Mask

Objectives/Concepts

1. To work with line, shape, and color.
2. To experiment with drawing technique.
3. To experiment with transfer drawing.
4. To work with symmetry.
5. To create pattern.

Technique

Drawing

Materials

18 in. oak tag circle
Oil crayons
Wooden ruler or craft stick

Alternate Materials

Markers, tempera paint

Activities/Process

1. Read or give a summary of the book *Why the Sun and the Moon Live in the Sky* by Elphinstone Dayrell, focusing on the illustrations.
2. Fold the circle in half.
3. On half the circle with black oil crayon, draw half a face using lines and shapes.
4. Draw shapes to make the sun rays on the same half of the oak tag.
5. Draw patterns or designs using only the same half of the oak tag.
6. Fold the paper in half again with the crayon lines inside.
7. With the edge of the craft stick or ruler, press against the oak tag rubbing back and forth over the entire piece, small areas at a time.

8. Open the oak tag and notice the impression of the crayon lines rubbed onto the other half.
9. Go over the lines with black oil crayon to darken them.
10. Color in the mask.

Questions for Discussion

What shapes did you use in your mask? How did you get the same thing on both sides of your mask? What did you have to be careful of? What is the sun? What is a folktale?

Share Time/Evaluation

_____

_____

_____

_____

Curriculum Connection

Science, Social Studies, Math, Language Arts, Music, Physical Education

Curriculum Extensions

Science: Research and learn about the sun, moon, ocean, and the animals that live in the water.

Social Studies: Locate Africa on a map. Find where Nigeria is located. Learn more about African tribes. Discuss masks and reasons for their use.

Math: Work with shapes and patterns.

Language Arts: Read or listen to other folktales. Invite a storyteller in or take a trip to the library to hear some stories. Make up your own folktale.

Music: Listen to African music.

Physical Education: Learn African dances.

Objectives/Concepts

1. To work with line, shape, and color.
2. To experiment with drawing technique.
3. To experiment with painting technique.
4. To experiment with printing technique.
5. To experiment with cutting and pasting technique.
6. To work with overlapping.
7. To create texture.

Technique

Drawing, Painting, Printing, Cutting
and Pasting

Materials

12 in. x 18 in. white paper
2 in. x 3 in. colored tissue paper
   (green varieties)
Brown crayon
Watercolor paints
Letter stamps for printing
Ink pad
Scissors
Glue

Alternate Materials

Markers, chalk, tempera paint, tissue paper, letters from newspaper, computer-generated letters

Activities/Process

1. Read or give a summary of the book *the alphabet tree* by Leo Lionni, focusing on the illustrations.
2. On white paper with brown crayon, draw a tree trunk with branches and limbs. Add some lines for the bark.
3. Paint the tree and the grass area around the tree with watercolor paints.

4. Cut leaves from the colored tissue paper by rounding one side and making a point on the other.
5. Glue leaves on the tree by overlapping them.
6. Print letters on top of the leaves.

Questions for Discussion

How did you show the texture of the tree? How did you make the shape of the leaves? What other colors did you use besides brown in your tree? How did you make many different varieties of the color green in the grass? What is printing? Why does the letter on the stamp look backwards?

Share Time/Evaluation

_____

_____

_____

_____

Curriculum Connection

Science, Math, Language Arts, Music

Curriculum Extensions

Science: Compare and contrast a variety of trees and leaves by noticing the color, shape, and size of each. Learn the parts of a tree and how a tree grows. Plant a tree. Go for a walk and observe trees. Gather leaves.

Math: Do math equations using leaves. Make charts of different kinds of trees or leaves that were seen on a walk. Estimate how many letters are in different length sentences then count them. Measure the length of different sentences.

Language Arts: Read other books about trees, leaves, and the alphabet. Make up words and sentences with letters. Do word searches, crossword puzzles, and other letter games.

Music: Sing alphabet songs.

The Foolish Tortoise

Turtle

Objectives/Concepts

1. To work with line, shape, and color.
2. To work with repetition.
3. To create pattern.
4. To experiment with painting technique.

Technique

Painting

Materials

12 in. x 18 in. white paper
Watercolor paints

Alternate Materials

Markers, chalk, tempera paint, construction paper, tissue paper

Activities/Process

1. Read or give a summary of the book *The Foolish Tortoise* by Richard Buckley, focusing on the illustrations.
2. On white paper with watercolors, paint a large turtle.
3. On the shell, repeat shapes to make a colorful pattern.
4. Try blending and mixing different colors.
5. Space around the turtle can be painted in for an environment.

Questions for Discussion

What is the difference between a turtle and a tortoise? What shape did you make for the turtle shell? What shapes did you use to create patterns in the shell? What colors did you use? What happened when you painted colors next to each other and they were still wet?

Share Time/Evaluation

_____

_____

_____

_____

Curriculum Connection

Science, Social Studies, Math, Language Arts, Physical Education

Curriculum Extensions

Science: Compare and contrast turtles and tortoises. Keep an aquarium in the classroom with a turtle as a class pet.

Social Studies: Find areas on the map where turtles and tortoises can be found.

Math: Create more patterns using drawing paper. Decorate walnut shells to represent the shells of turtles and use them to add and subtract.

Language Arts: Read other books about a turtle or a tortoise. Talk about the story of the tortoise and the hare and have students explain the moral of the story. Write a poem.

Physical Education: Pretend that you are a turtle and have a race against someone else.

Wild Thing

Objectives/Concepts

1. To work with line, shape, and color.
2. To experiment with drawing technique.
3. To experiment with painting technique.
4. To experiment with color mixing.
5. To create texture.

Technique

Drawing, Painting

Materials

12 in. x 18 in. white paper
Fine-line permanent black marker
Watercolor paints

Alternate Materials

Crayons, colored pencils, scratch board

Activities/Process

1. Read or give a summary of the book *Where the Wild Things Are* by Maurice Sendak, focusing on the illustrations.
2. On white paper with marker, draw a large wild thing. Add horns, teeth, claws, fur, hair, clothing, and other details to show texture.
3. Paint with watercolor paints.

Questions for Discussion

What shapes did you use to make the wild thing? What colors did you use to make other colors? What happened when you painted colors next to each other and they were still wet? Where did you show texture? How did you make the texture and what does it look like it would feel like?

Curriculum Extensions

Science: Compare and contrast different kinds of forests. Take a field trip to a forest. Plant some trees and watch them grow.

Social Studies: On a world map, find, label, and color in the oceans. Locate large forest areas.

Math: Plant seedlings of trees and measure their growth. Chart different types of trees found in the area where you live.

Language Arts: Make up your own story about a wild thing. Tell or write a story about sailing to a faraway land and the adventures you have.

Music: Listen to music from other lands.

Physical Education: Pretend to be wild things and play tag. Have a controlled rumpus in the gym.

Woven Scarecrow

Objectives/Concepts

1. To work with line, shape, and color.
2. To create texture.
3. To experience weaving.
4. To create pattern.
5. To work with fringing.
6. To experiment with cutting and pasting technique.

Technique

Cutting and Pasting

Materials

4½ in. x 6 in. colored paper (2 per student)
¼ in. x 6 in. strips of colored paper
Assorted colored paper scraps
Scissors
Glue
Buttons

Alternate Materials

Markers, crayons (wax or oil), scraps of material, dried hay

Activities/Process

1. Read or give a summary of the book *The Little Scarecrow Boy* by Margaret Wise Brown, focusing on the illustrations.
2. In the middle of one 4½ in. x 6 in. paper, cut several slits about ¼ in. apart. Leave ¼ in. uncut border around all edges.
3. Weave the ¼ in. x 6 in. strips through the slits in an under-and-over pattern, alternating every other row.
4. Add colored paper rectangles for arms.

5. With the other 4½ in. x 6 in. paper, create pant legs by cutting away a triangle shape from one of the 4½ in. sides. Glue the pants to the shirt.
6. Pockets, belts, patches, and other details can be added with colored paper or other materials.
7. Cut a circle or oval for the head and add facial features. Buttons can be used for the eyes.
8. Glue the head to the body.
9. Cut paper fringe to resemble hay and glue to the bottom of the sleeves, pants, and neck areas.
10. A bird can be cut and glued onto the shoulder of the scarecrow.

Questions for Discussion

Why do we have scarecrows? What are scarecrows usually made of? What is weaving? Are there different kinds of weaving? How did you show texture in your picture?

Share Time/Evaluation

_____
_____
_____
_____

Curriculum Connection

Science, Math, Language Arts, Physical Education

Curriculum Extensions

Science: Discuss farming and gardening. Plant a small garden either in the classroom or around the schoolyard. Compare and contrast different kinds of seeds.

Math: Graph favorite vegetables. Estimate how many seeds are in a glass jar. Use seeds for adding and subtracting.

Language Arts: Read other books about scarecrows, farming, and gardening. Pretend that you are a scarecrow and tell a story.

Physical Education: Pretend that you are a scarecrow. Hold very still in different positions, then try blowing in the wind.

Conclusion

Throughout this book, children are introduced to various materials and methods in art. They are able to focus on personal meaning and are encouraged to use their knowledge and skills to express their individuality. Discovery through observation is emphasized, and children are encouraged to experience their world through ideas, feelings, and interests. The lessons in this book allow children to respond to the art of illustrations in children's books and then create their own art. Picture books can be utilized as a comfortable motivation. Children should be encouraged to make connections with everyday life and the world around them.

Illustrations have a strong impact, and they have the capability of informing as eloquently as any prose. Children learn to appreciate the various styles of art in illustrations, and they enjoy reading the pictures and sharing something fascinating about them, both verbally and visually.

The activities in this book correlate to critical thinking skills. Children are given the opportunity to recall what they already know about the lesson by giving examples from their surroundings as well as from their experiences, and then apply the information to new situations. They are able to observe and give descriptions of the visuals presented. Education involves instruction, and some type of depiction of what is being taught must supplement the oral instruction of a teacher. Discussion questions allow for critical thinking skills, and by emphasizing the elements and principles in the lesson, the children are able to more deeply comprehend.

Creating art allows synthesis through application. An understanding of how illustrators use compositional elements and principles in their creation of children's books assists children in their own creative work. Some illustrations are realistic, connecting children with the lives they know. Other illustrations exist in the realm of fantasy, which allows for a more fanciful imaginative response. Either way, children relate to books and their illustrations, and there is a great connection between literature and art. Books capture children's attention and engage their imagination. They become excited and want to communicate their enthusiasm, which can be accomplished through an art activity. Besides the connection of art and literature, art lessons can incorporate all areas of classroom studies.

Appendix A

Art Materials

The following materials are used throughout the various art lessons in this book or as alternate materials. Additional materials may be used as a result of individual creativity. The materials listed are safe for children; however, adult supervision is always recommended when young children are working. Safety precautions should be utilized when children are cutting, stapling, or using sharp objects.

Aluminum foil
Beads
Brayer
Brushes
Buttons
Cellophane
Chalk
Charcoal
Charcoal pencils
Clay
Colored pencils
Cotton swabs
Craft eyes
Crayons
  oil
  wax
Fabric scraps
Feathers
Foam board
Glitter
Glue
Hole punch
Ink pads
Inking plate
Magazines

Markers
  fine-line
  permanent
  washable
Masking tape
Nature items
Newspaper
Oak tag
Paint
  acrylic
  tempera
  watercolor
Paintbrushes
Paper
  brown wrapping
  construction
  corrugated
  crepe
  gift wrapping
  metallic
  textured
  tissue
  wallpaper
  watercolor
  white drawing

Paper clips
Paper towels
Pastels (chalk)
Pen (ball point)
Pencil
Pipe cleaner
Printing plate
Ribbon
Ruler
Scissors
  straight-edged
  fancy-edged
Sponges
Stapler
Sticky dots
Straws
String
Styrofoam
  packing
  sheet
Toothpicks
Wood scraps
Yarn

Appendix B

*A*ctivity *Charts*

For quick reference, the activities listed are arranged in alphabetical order by title. Motivational books have been listed; however, other books could be used that are based on the same subject. Depending upon the level of the students participating, the vocabulary and skill expectations can be simplified or enhanced and need not be subjected to the level given in the sample. Technique might also be changed if alternate materials are being used. Therefore, it is important that the supervisors using this chart and the activities in this book realize that the more flexible they are in setting up and presenting the activities, the more satisfied they will be with the creativity and learning results of the children involved. Utilization of the sample activities presented in this book as a pivoting point for individual classroom curricula allows for modification of subject themes, classroom levels, and materials on hand, and curriculum study.

Guide to Chart Abbreviations

Level: E (easy), M (moderate), A (advanced)

Technique: D (drawing), P (painting), Pr (printing),
C and P (cutting and pasting), S (sculpture)

Curriculum Connection: M (math), LA (language arts), S (science),
SS (social studies), PE (physical education),
Mu (music)

Activity Chart: Overview

Activity Title	Level	Technique	Curriculum Connection	Page Number
Alligator	E	C and P	S, SS, M, LA, Mu, PE	5
Baby Owls	E	Pr, C and P	S, SS, M, LA, Mu, PE	7
Bear in Two Styles	M	D	S, SS, M, LA, Mu, PE	9
Bird with Apple	E	D, P, C and P	S, M, LA, Mu, PE	11
Blanket Design	E	C and P	S, SS, M, LA, Mu, PE	13
Brown Bear	M	Pr, C and P	S, SS, M, LA, Mu, PE	15
Butterfly	E	D, C and P	S, M, LA, PE	17
Cat	A	D, Pr	S, M, LA	19
Caterpillar	E	P, C and P	S, M, LA, Mu, PE	21
Chameleon	M	D, P, Pr	S, SS, M, LA, PE	23
City Buildings	M	C and P	S, SS, M, LA, Mu	25
Clay Dragon	E	S	S, SS, M, LA, Mu, PE	27
Clown	E	D	S, SS, M, LA, Mu, PE	29
Colorful Elephant	E	D, C and P	S, SS, M, LA, PE	31
Colorful Patterned Fish	E	C and P	S, SS, M, LA, Mu, PE	33
Constellations	A	D, C and P	S, M, LA, Mu	35
Crazy Quilt	M	D, C and P	SS, M, LA	37
Dalmatian	E	Pr, C and P	S, SS, M, LA, Mu, PE	39
Dragon	E	D, P	S, SS, M, LA, Mu, PE	41
Elephant	E	S	S, SS, M, LA, PE	43
Fall Leaves	E	D, P	S, SS, M, LA, PE	45
Fall Tree	A	D, C and P	S, SS, M, LA, Mu	47
Flowers in Vase	E	D, C and P	S, SS, M, LA	49
Flying Bird	M	P, C and P	S, SS, M, LA, Mu, PE	51
Fruit and Vegetable Still Life	E	D, C and P	S, SS, M, LA	53
Gingerbread Man	E	D, P, C and P	S, SS, M, LA, Mu, PE	55
Giraffe with Neckties	M	D, C and P	S, SS, M, LA	57
Hand Design	E	D, C and P	S, SS, M, LA, Mu	59
Hat Collage	A	D, C and P	SS, LA, PE	61
Hen	M	C and P	S, SS, M, LA, Mu, PE	63
Hot Air Balloon	M	D, C and P, S	S, SS, M, LA, Mu	65
Jack-in-the-Box	M	C and P	S, SS, M, LA, Mu, PE	67
Jungle or Rain Forest Scene	M	D, P	S, SS, M, LA, Mu, PE	69
Ladybugs	E	P	S, SS, M, LA, Mu	71
Merry-Go-Round Horse	A	D, C and P, S	S, SS, M, LA, Mu, PE	73
Monster	E	D	SS, LA, PE	75
Mouse in Attic	A	C and P	S, SS, M, LA, Mu, PE	77
Panda Bear	E	P	S, SS, M, LA, Mu, PE	79
Parrot	E	D	S, SS, M, LA, Mu, PE	81
Patriotic Parade	A	D, Pr, C and P	S, SS, M, LA, Mu, PE	83
Printed Fish	E	P, Pr, C and P	S, M, LA, Mu, PE	85
Raven	A	P, C and P	S, SS, M, LA, Mu, PE	87
Reading a Book	M	D, C and P	S, SS, M, LA, Mu	89
Roller Coaster	M	C and P, S	S, SS, M, LA, Mu, PE	91
School Bus	E	D	S, SS, M, LA, Mu	93
Sea Glass and Shells in a Bottle	A	D, P, C and P	S, SS, M, LA, Mu, PE	95
Skeletons	A	D, C and P	S, M, LA, Mu, PE	97
Snail Design	E	D, P	S, SS, M, LA, PE	99
Snail in an Environment	M	D, P, C and P	S, SS, M, LA, PE	101

Activity Chart: Overview *(concluded)*

Activity Title	Level	Technique	Curriculum Connection	Page Number
Snake	M	P	S, SS, M, LA, PE	103
Snowman	M	D, Pr, C and P	S, SS, M, LA, PE	105
Spider	M	C and P	S, M, LA, Mu	107
Sun and Moon Mobile	A	C and P, S	S, SS, M, LA, Mu, PE	109
Sun Mask	M	D	S, SS, M, LA, Mu, PE	111
Tree with Letters	M	D, P, Pr, C and P	S, M, LA, Mu	113
Turtle	E	P	S, SS, M, LA, PE	115
Wild Thing	M	D, P	S, SS, M, LA, Mu, PE	117
Woven Scarecrow	A	C and P	S, M, LA, PE	119

Activity Chart: Level

Activity Title by Level	Technique	Curriculum Connection	Page Number

Easy

Alligator	C and P	S, SS, M, LA, Mu, PE	5
Baby Owls	Pr, C and P	S, SS, M, LA, Mu, PE	7
Bird with Apple	D, P, C and P	S, M, LA, Mu, PE	11
Blanket Design	C and P	S, SS, M, LA, Mu, PE	13
Butterfly	D, C and P	S, M, LA, PE	17
Caterpillar	P, C and P	S, M, LA, Mu, PE	21
Clay Dragon	S	S, SS, M, LA, Mu, PE	27
Clown	D	S, SS, M, LA, Mu, PE	29
Colorful Elephant	D, C and P	S, SS, M, LA, PE	31
Colorful Patterned Fish	C and P	S, SS, M, LA, Mu, PE	33
Dalmatian	Pr, C and P	S, SS, M, LA, Mu, PE	39
Dragon	D, P	S, SS, M, LA, Mu, PE	41
Elephant	S	S, SS, M, LA, PE	43
Fall Leaves	D, P	S, SS, M, LA, PE	45
Flowers in Vase	D, C and P	S, SS, M, LA	49
Fruit and Vegetable Still Life	D, C and P	S, SS, M, LA	53
Gingerbread Man	D, P, C and P	S, SS, M, LA, Mu, PE	55
Hand Design	D, C and P	S, SS, M, LA, Mu	59
Ladybugs	P	S, SS, M, LA, Mu	71
Monster	D	SS, LA, PE	75
Panda Bear	P	S, SS, M, LA, Mu, PE	79
Parrot	D	S, SS, M, LA, Mu, PE	81
Printed Fish	P, Pr, C and P	S, M, LA, Mu, PE	85
School Bus	D	S, SS, M, LA, Mu	93
Snail Design	D, P	S, SS, M, LA, PE	99
Turtle	P	S, SS, M, LA, PE	115

Moderate

Bear in Two Styles	D	S, SS, M, LA, Mu, PE	9
Brown Bear	Pr, C and P	S, SS, M, LA, Mu, PE	15
Chameleon	D, P, Pr	S, SS, M, LA, PE	23
City Buildings	C and P	S, SS, M, LA, Mu	25
Crazy Quilt	D, C and P	SS, M, LA	37
Flying Bird	P, C and P	S, SS, M, LA, Mu, PE	51
Giraffe with Neckties	D, C and P	S, SS, M, LA	57
Hen	C and P	S, M, LA, Mu, PE	63
Hot Air Balloon	D, C and P, S	S, SS, M, LA, Mu	65
Jack-in-the-Box	C and P	S, SS, M, LA, Mu, PE	67
Jungle or Rain Forest Scene	D, P	S, SS, M, LA, Mu, PE	69
Reading a Book	D, C and P	S, SS, M, LA, Mu	89
Roller Coaster	C and P, S	S, SS, M, LA, Mu, PE	91
Snail in an Environment	D, P, C and P	S, SS, M, LA, PE	101
Snake	P	S, SS, M, LA, PE	103
Snowman	D, Pr, C and P	S, SS, M, LA, PE	105
Spider	C and P	S, M, LA, Mu	107
Sun Mask	D	S, SS, M, LA, Mu, PE	111
Tree with Letters	D, P, Pr, C and P	S, M, LA, Mu	113
Wild Thing	D, P	S, SS, M, LA, Mu, PE	117

Activity Chart: Level *(concluded)*

Activity Title by Level	Technique	Curriculum Connection	Page Number
Advanced			
Cat	D, Pr	S, M, LA	19
Constellations	D, C and P	S, M, LA, Mu	35
Fall Tree	D, C and P	S, SS, M, LA, Mu	47
Hat Collage	D, C and P	SS, LA, PE	61
Merry-Go-Round Horse	D, C and P, S	S, SS, M, LA, Mu, PE	73
Mouse in Attic	C and P	S, SS, M, LA, Mu, PE	77
Patriotic Parade	D, Pr, C and P	S, SS, M, LA, Mu, PE	83
Raven	P, C and P	S, SS, M, LA, Mu, PE	87
Sea Glass and Shells in a Bottle	D, P, C and P	S, SS, M, LA, Mu, PE	95
Skeletons	D, C and P	S, M, LA, Mu, PE	97
Sun and Moon Mobile	C and P, S	S, SS, M, LA, Mu, PE	109
Woven Scarecrow	C and P	S, M, LA, PE	119

Activity Chart: Technique

Activity Title by Technique	Level	Curriculum Connection	Page Number
Drawing			
Bear in Two Styles	M	S, SS, M, LA, Mu, PE	9
Bird with Apple	E	S, M, LA, Mu, PE	11
Butterfly	E	S, M, LA, PE	17
Cat	A	S, M, LA	19
Chameleon	M	S, SS, M, LA, PE	23
Clown	E	S, SS, M, LA, Mu, PE	29
Colorful Elephant	E	S, SS, M, LA, PE	31
Constellations	A	S, M, LA, Mu	35
Crazy Quilt	M	SS, M, LA	37
Dragon	E	S, SS, M, LA, Mu, PE	41
Fall Leaves	E	S, SS, M, LA, PE	45
Fall Tree	A	S, SS, M, LA, Mu	47
Flowers in Vase	E	S, SS, M, LA	49
Fruit and Vegetable Still Life	E	S, SS, M, LA	53
Gingerbread Man	E	S, SS, M, LA, Mu, PE	55
Giraffe with Neckties	M	S, SS, M, LA	57
Hand Design	E	S, SS, M, LA, Mu	59
Hat Collage	A	SS, LA, PE	61
Hot Air Balloon	M	S, SS, M, LA, Mu	65
Jungle or Rain Forest Scene	M	S, SS, M, LA, Mu, PE	69
Merry-Go-Round Horse	A	S, SS, M, LA, Mu, PE	73
Monster	E	SS, LA, PE	75
Parrot	E	S, SS, M, LA, Mu, PE	81
Patriotic Parade	A	S, SS, M, LA, Mu, PE	83
Reading a Book	M	S, SS, M, LA, Mu	89
School Bus	E	S, SS, M, LA, Mu	93
Sea Glass and Shells in a Bottle	A	S, SS, M, LA, Mu, PE	95
Skeletons	A	S, M, LA, Mu, PE	97
Snail Design	E	S, SS, M, LA, PE	99
Snail in an Environment	M	S, SS, M, LA, PE	101
Snowman	M	S, SS, M, LA, PE	105
Sun Mask	M	S, SS, M, LA, Mu, PE	111
Tree with Letters	M	S, M, LA, Mu	113
Wild Thing	M	S, SS, M, LA, Mu, PE	117
Painting			
Bird with Apple	E	S, M, LA, Mu, PE	11
Caterpillar	E	S, M, LA, Mu, PE	21
Chameleon	M	S, SS, M, LA, PE	23
Dragon	E	S, SS, M, LA, Mu, PE	41
Fall Leaves	E	S, SS, M, LA, PE	45
Flying Bird	M	S, SS, M, LA, Mu, PE	51
Gingerbread Man	E	S, SS, M, LA, Mu, PE	55
Jungle or Rain Forest Scene	M	S, SS, M, LA, Mu, PE	69
Ladybugs	E	S, SS, M, LA, Mu	71
Panda Bear	E	S, SS, M, LA, Mu, PE	79
Printed Fish	E	S, M, LA, Mu, PE	85
Raven	A	S, SS, M, LA, Mu, PE	87

Activity Chart: Technique *(continued)*

Activity Title by Technique	Level	Curriculum Connection	Page Number
Painting *(concluded)*			
Sea Glass and Shells in a Bottle	A	S, SS, M, LA, Mu, PE	95
Snail Design	E	S, SS, M, LA, PE	99
Snail in an Environment	M	S, SS, M, LA, PE	101
Snake	M	S, SS, M, LA, PE	103
Tree with Letters	M	S, M, LA, Mu	113
Turtle	E	S, SS, M, LA, PE	115
Wild Thing	M	S, SS, M, LA, Mu, PE	117
Printing			
Baby Owls	E	S, SS, M, LA, Mu, PE	7
Brown Bear	M	S, SS, M, LA, Mu, PE	15
Cat	A	S, M, LA	19
Chameleon	M	S, SS, M, LA, PE	23
Dalmatian	E	S, SS, M, LA, Mu, PE	39
Patriotic Parade	A	S, SS, M, LA, Mu, PE	83
Printed Fish	E	S, M, LA, Mu, PE	85
Snowman	M	S, SS, M, LA, PE	105
Tree with Letters	M	S, M, LA, Mu	113
Cutting and Pasting			
Alligator	E	S, SS, M, LA, Mu, PE	5
Baby Owls	E	S, SS, M, LA, Mu, PE	7
Bird with Apple	E	S, M, LA, Mu, PE	11
Blanket Design	E	S, SS, M, LA, Mu, PE	13
Brown Bear	M	S, SS, M, LA, Mu, PE	15
Butterfly	E	S, M, LA, PE	17
Caterpillar	E	S, M, LA, Mu, PE	21
City Buildings	M	S, SS, M, LA, Mu	25
Colorful Elephant	E	S, SS, M, LA, PE	31
Colorful Patterned Fish	E	S, SS, M, LA, Mu, PE	33
Constellations	A	S, M, LA, Mu	35
Crazy Quilt	M	SS, M, LA	37
Dalmatian	E	S, SS, M, LA, Mu, PE	39
Fall Tree	A	S, SS, M, LA, Mu	47
Flowers in Vase	E	S, SS, M, LA	49
Flying Bird	M	S, SS, M, LA, Mu, PE	51
Fruit and Vegetable Still Life	E	S, SS, M, LA	53
Gingerbread Man	E	S, SS, M, LA, Mu, PE	55
Giraffe with Neckties	M	S, SS, M, LA	57
Hand Design	E	S, SS, M, LA, Mu	59
Hat Collage	A	SS, LA, PE	61
Hen	M	S, SS, M, LA, Mu, PE	63
Hot Air Balloon	M	S, SS, M, LA, Mu	65
Jack-in-the-Box	M	S, SS, M, LA, Mu, PE	67
Merry-Go-Round Horse	A	S, SS, M, LA, Mu, PE	73
Mouse in Attic	A	S, SS, M, LA, Mu, PE	77
Patriotic Parade	A	S, SS, M, LA, Mu, PE	83

(continued)

Activity Chart: Technique *(concluded)*

Activity Title by Technique	Level	Curriculum Connection	Page Number
Cutting and Pasting *(concluded)*			
Printed Fish	E	S, M, LA, Mu, PE	85
Raven	A	S, SS, M, LA, Mu, PE	87
Reading a Book	M	S, SS, M, LA, Mu	89
Roller Coaster	M	S, SS, M, LA, Mu, PE	91
Sea Glass and Shells in a Bottle	A	S, SS, M, LA, Mu, PE	95
Skeletons	A	S, M, LA, Mu, PE	97
Snail in an Environment	M	S, SS, M, LA, PE	101
Snowman	M	S, SS, M, LA, PE	105
Spider	M	S, M, LA, Mu	107
Sun and Moon Mobile	A	S, SS, M, LA, Mu, PE	109
Tree with Letters	M	S, M, LA, Mu	113
Woven Scarecrow	A	S, M, LA, PE	119
Sculpture			
Clay Dragon	E	S, SS, M, LA, Mu, PE	27
Elephant	E	S, SS, M, LA, PE	43
Hot Air Balloon	M	S, SS, M, LA, Mu	65
Merry-Go-Round Horse	A	S, SS, M, LA, Mu, PE	73
Roller Coaster	M	S, SS, M, LA, Mu, PE	91
Sun and Moon Mobile	A	S, SS, M, LA, Mu, PE	109

Activity Chart: Curriculum Extensions

Activity Title by Curriculum Extension	Level	Technique	Page Number
Science			
Alligator	E	C and P	5
Baby Owls	E	Pr, C and P	7
Bear in Two Styles	M	D	9
Bird with Apple	E	D, P, C and P	11
Blanket Design	E	C and P	13
Brown Bear	M	Pr, C and P	15
Butterfly	E	D, C and P	17
Cat	A	D, Pr	19
Caterpillar	E	P, C and P	21
Chameleon	M	D, P, Pr	23
City Buildings	M	C and P	25
Clay Dragon	E	S	27
Clown	E	D	29
Colorful Elephant	E	D, C and P	31
Colorful Patterned Fish	E	C and P	33
Constellations	A	D, C and P	35
Dalmatian	E	Pr, C and P	39
Dragon	E	D, P	41
Elephant	E	S	43
Fall Leaves	E	D, P	45
Fall Tree	A	D, C and P	47
Flowers in Vase	E	D, C and P	49
Flying Bird	M	P, C and P	51
Fruit and Vegetable Still Life	E	D, C and P	53
Gingerbread Man	E	D, P, C and P	55
Giraffe with Neckties	M	D, C and P	57
Hand Design	E	D, C and P	59
Hen	M	C and P	63
Hot Air Balloon	M	D, C and P, S	65
Jack-in-the-Box	M	C and P	67
Jungle or Rain Forest Scene	M	D, P	69
Ladybugs	E	P	71
Merry-Go-Round Horse	A	D, C and P, S	73
Mouse in Attic	A	C and P	77
Panda Bear	E	P	79
Parrot	E	D	81
Patriotic Parade	A	D, Pr, C and P	83
Printed Fish	E	P, Pr, C and P	85
Raven	A	P, C and P	87
Reading a Book	M	D, C and P	89
Roller Coaster	M	C and P, S	91
School Bus	E	D	93
Sea Glass and Shells in a Bottle	A	D, P, C and P	95
Skeletons	A	D, C and P	97
Snail Design	E	D, P	99
Snail in an Environment	M	D, P, C and P	101
Snake	M	P	103

(continued)

Activity Chart: Curriculum Extensions (continued)

Activity Title by Curriculum Extension	Level	Technique	Page Number
Science (concluded)			
Snowman	M	D, Pr, C and P	105
Spider	M	C and P	107
Sun and Moon Mobile	A	C and P, S	109
Sun Mask	M	D	111
Tree with Letters	M	D, P, Pr, C and P	113
Turtle	E	P	115
Wild Thing	M	D, P	117
Woven Scarecrow	A	C and P	119
Social Studies			
Alligator	E	C and P	5
Baby Owls	E	Pr, C and P	7
Bear in Two Styles	M	D	9
Blanket Design	E	C and P	13
Brown Bear	M	Pr, C and P	15
Chameleon	M	D, P, Pr	23
City Buildings	M	C and P	25
Clay Dragon	E	S	27
Clown	E	D	29
Colorful Elephant	E	D, C and P	31
Colorful Patterned Fish	E	C and P	33
Crazy Quilt	M	D, C and P	37
Dalmatian	E	Pr, C and P	39
Dragon	E	D, P	41
Elephant	E	S	43
Fall Leaves	E	D, P	45
Fall Tree	A	D, C and P	47
Flowers in Vase	E	D, C and P	49
Flying Bird	M	P, C and P	51
Fruit and Vegetable Still Life	E	D, C and P	53
Gingerbread Man	E	D, P, C and P	55
Giraffe with Neckties	M	D, C and P	57
Hand Design	E	D, C and P	59
Hat Collage	A	D, C and P	61
Hen	M	C and P	63
Hot Air Balloon	M	D, C and P, S	65
Jack-in-the-Box	M	C and P	67
Jungle or Rain Forest Scene	M	D, P	69
Ladybugs	E	P	71
Merry-Go-Round Horse	A	D, C and P, S	73
Monster	E	D	75
Mouse in Attic	A	C and P	77
Panda Bear	E	P	79
Parrot	E	D	81
Patriotic Parade	A	D, Pr, C and P	83
Raven	A	P, C and P	87
Reading a Book	M	D, C and P	89
Roller Coaster	M	C and P, S	91

Activity Chart: Curriculum Extensions *(continued)*

Activity Title by Curriculum Extension	Level	Technique	Page Number
Social Studies *(concluded)*			
School Bus	E	D	93
Sea Glass and Shells in a Bottle	A	D, P, C and P	95
Snail Design	E	D, P	99
Snail in an Environment	M	D, P, C and P	101
Snake	M	P	103
Snowman	M	D, Pr, C and P	105
Sun and Moon Mobile	A	C and P, S	109
Sun Mask	M	D	111
Turtle	E	P	115
Wild Thing	M	D, P	117
Math			
Alligator	E	C and P	5
Baby Owls	E	Pr, C and P	7
Bear in Two Styles	M	D	9
Bird with Apple	E	D, P, C and P	11
Blanket Design	E	C and P	13
Brown Bear	M	Pr, C and P	15
Butterfly	E	D, C and P	17
Cat	A	D, Pr	19
Caterpillar	E	P, C and P	21
Chameleon	M	D, P, Pr	23
City Buildings	M	C and P	25
Clay Dragon	E	S	27
Clown	E	D	29
Colorful Elephant	E	D, C and P	31
Colorful Patterned Fish	E	C and P	33
Constellations	A	D, C and P	35
Crazy Quilt	M	D, C and P	37
Dalmatian	E	Pr, C and P	39
Dragon	E	D, P	41
Elephant	E	S	43
Fall Leaves	E	D, P	45
Fall Tree	A	D, C and P	47
Flowers in Vase	E	D, C and P	49
Flying Bird	M	P, C and P	51
Fruit and Vegetable Still Life	E	D, C and P	53
Gingerbread Man	E	D, P, C and P	55
Giraffe with Neckties	M	D, C and P	57
Hand Design	E	D, C and P	59
Hen	M	C and P	63
Hot Air Balloon	M	D, C and P, S	65
Jack-in-the-Box	M	C and P	67
Jungle or Rain Forest Scene	M	D, P	69
Ladybugs	E	P	71
Merry-Go-Round Horse	A	D, C and P, S	73
Mouse in Attic	A	C and P	77

(continued)

Activity Chart: Curriculum Extensions (continued)

Activity Title by Curriculum Extension	Level	Technique	Page Number
Math (concluded)			
Panda Bear	E	P	79
Parrot	E	D	81
Patriotic Parade	A	D, Pr, C and P	83
Printed Fish	E	P, Pr, C and P	85
Raven	A	P, C and P	87
Reading a Book	M	D, C and P	89
Roller Coaster	M	C and P, S	91
School Bus	E	D	93
Sea Glass and Shells in a Bottle	A	D, P, C and P	95
Skeletons	A	D, C and P	97
Snail Design	E	D, P	99
Snail in an Environment	M	D, P, C and P	101
Snake	M	P	103
Snowman	M	D, Pr, C and P	105
Spider	M	C and P	107
Sun and Moon Mobile	A	C and P, S	109
Sun Mask	M	D	111
Tree with Letters	M	D, P, Pr, C and P	113
Turtle	E	P	115
Wild Thing	M	D, P	117
Woven Scarecrow	A	C and P	119
Language Arts			
Alligator	E	C and P	5
Baby Owls	E	Pr, C and P	7
Bear in Two Styles	M	D	9
Bird with Apple	E	D, P, C and P	11
Blanket Design	E	C and P	13
Brown Bear	M	Pr, C and P	15
Butterfly	E	D, C and P	17
Cat	A	D, Pr	19
Caterpillar	E	P, C and P	21
Chameleon	M	D, P, Pr	23
City Buildings	M	C and P	25
Clay Dragon	E	S	27
Clown	E	D	29
Colorful Elephant	E	D, C and P	31
Colorful Patterned Fish	E	C and P	33
Constellations	A	D, C and P	35
Crazy Quilt	M	D, C and P	37
Dalmatian	E	Pr, C and P	39
Dragon	E	D, P	41
Elephant	E	S	43
Fall Leaves	E	D, P	45
Fall Tree	A	D, C and P	47
Flowers in Vase	E	D, C and P	49
Flying Bird	M	P, C and P	51
Fruit and Vegetable Still Life	E	D, C and P	53

Activity Chart: Curriculum Extensions *(continued)*

Activity Title by Curriculum Extension	Level	Technique	Page Number
Language Arts *(concluded)*			
Gingerbread Man	E	D, P, C and P	55
Giraffe with Neckties	M	D, C and P	57
Hand Design	E	D, C and P	59
Hat Collage	A	D, C and P	61
Hen	M	C and P	63
Hot Air Balloon	M	D, C and P, S	65
Jack-in-the-Box	M	C and P	67
Jungle or Rain Forest Scene	M	D, P	69
Ladybugs	E	P	71
Merry-Go-Round Horse	A	D, C and P, S	73
Monster	E	D	75
Mouse in Attic	A	C and P	77
Panda Bear	E	P	79
Parrot	E	D	81
Patriotic Parade	A	D, Pr, C and P	83
Printed Fish	E	P, Pr, C and P	85
Raven	A	P, C and P	87
Reading a Book	M	D, C and P	89
Roller Coaster	M	C and P, S	91
School Bus	E	D	93
Sea Glass and Shells in a Bottle	A	D, P, C and P	95
Skeletons	A	D, C and P	97
Snail Design	E	D, P	99
Snail in an Environment	M	D, P, C and P	101
Snake	M	P	103
Snowman	M	D, Pr, C and P	105
Spider	M	C and P	107
Sun and Moon Mobile	A	C and P, S	109
Sun Mask	M	D	111
Tree with Letters	M	D, P, Pr, C and P	113
Turtle	E	P	115
Wild Thing	M	D, P	117
Woven Scarecrow	A	C and P	119
Music			
Alligator	E	C and P	5
Baby Owls	E	Pr, C and P	7
Bear in Two Styles	M	D	9
Bird with Apple	E	D, P, C and P	11
Blanket Design	E	C and P	13
Brown Bear	M	Pr, C and P	15
Caterpillar	E	P, C and P	21
City Buildings	M	C and P	25
Clay Dragon	E	S	27
Clown	E	D	29
Colorful Patterned Fish	E	C and P	33
Constellations	A	C and P	35

(continued)

Activity Chart: Curriculum Extensions *(continued)*

Activity Title by Curriculum Extension	Level	Technique	Page Number
Music *(concluded)*			
Dalmatian	E	Pr, C and P	39
Dragon	E	D, P	41
Fall Tree	A	D, C and P	47
Flying Bird	M	P, C and P	51
Gingerbread Man	E	D, P, C and P	55
Hand Design	E	D, C and P	59
Hen	M	C and P	63
Hot Air Balloon	M	D, C and P, S	65
Jack-in-the-Box	M	C and P	67
Jungle or Rain Forest Scene	M	D, P	69
Ladybugs	E	P	71
Merry-Go-Round Horse	A	D, C and P, S	73
Mouse in Attic	A	C and P	77
Panda Bear	E	P	79
Parrot	E	D	81
Patriotic Parade	A	D, Pr, C and P	83
Printed Fish	E	P, Pr, C and P	85
Raven	A	P, C and P	87
Reading a Book	M	D, C and P	89
Roller Coaster	M	C and P, S	91
School Bus	E	D	93
Sea Glass and Shells in a Bottle	A	D, P, C and P	95
Skeletons	A	D, C and P	97
Spider	M	C and P	107
Sun and Moon Mobile	A	C and P, S	109
Sun Mask	M	D	111
Tree with Letters	M	D, P, Pr, C and P	113
Wild Thing	M	D, P	117
Physical Education			
Alligator	E	C and P	5
Baby Owls	E	Pr, C and P	7
Bear in Two Styles	M	D	9
Bird with Apple	E	D, P, C and P	11
Blanket Design	E	C and P	13
Brown Bear	M	Pr, C and P	15
Butterfly	E	D, C and P	17
Caterpillar	E	P, C and P	21
Chameleon	M	D, P, Pr	23
Clay Dragon	E	S	27
Clown	E	D	29
Colorful Elephant	E	D, C and P	31
Colorful Patterned Fish	E	C and P	33
Dalmatian	E	Pr, C and P	39
Dragon	E	D, P	41
Elephant	E	S	43
Fall Leaves	E	D, P	45
Flying Bird	M	P, C and P	51

Activity Chart: Curriculum Extensions *(concluded)*

Activity Title by Curriculum Extension	Level	Technique	Page Number
Physical Education *(concluded)*			
Gingerbread Man	E	D, P, C and P	55
Hat Collage	A	D, C and P	61
Hen	M	C and P	63
Jack-in-the-Box	M	C and P	67
Jungle or Rain Forest Scene	M	D, P	69
Merry-Go-Round Horse	A	D, C and P, S	73
Monster	E	D	75
Mouse in Attic	A	C and P	77
Panda Bear	E	P	79
Parrot	E	D	81
Patriotic Parade	A	D, Pr, C and P	83
Printed Fish	E	P, Pr, C and P	85
Raven	A	P, C and P	87
Roller Coaster	M	C and P, S	91
Sea Glass and Shells in a Bottle	A	D, P, C and P	95
Skeletons	A	D, C and P	97
Snail Design	E	D, P	99
Snail in an Environment	M	D, P, C and P	101
Snake	M	P	103
Snowman	M	D, Pr, C and P	105
Sun and Moon Mobile	A	C and P, S	109
Sun Mask	M	D	111
Turtle	E	P	115
Wild Thing	M	D, P	117
Woven Scarecrow	A	C and P	119

Appendix C

$\mathcal{B}$ook List Information

Alphabetically by author's last name

Title	Author	Illustrator	Publisher	Copyright
Funnybones	Janet and Allan Ahlberg	Janet and Allan Ahlberg	Scholastic, Inc.	1980
Keep Your Mouth Closed, Dear	Aliki	Aliki	Pied Piper	1966
Hide and Snake	Keith Baker	Keith Baker	Trumpet Club	1991
Animals Should Definitely <u>Not</u> Wear Clothing	Judi Barrett	Ron Barrett	Scholastic, Inc.	1970
Too Many Books	Caroline Feller Bauer	Diane Paterson	Puffin Books	1986
The Snowman	Raymond Briggs		Random House	1978
The Little Scarecrow Boy	Margaret Wise Brown	David Diaz	Harper Collins	1998
The Foolish Tortoise	Richard Buckley	Eric Carle	Picture Book Studio	1985
Hot-Air Henry	Mary Calhoun	Erick Ingraham	William Morrow and Company	1981
The Grouchy Ladybug	Eric Carle	Eric Carle	Scholastic, Inc.	1977
The Very Busy Spider	Eric Carle	Eric Carle	Philomel Books	1984
The Very Hungry Caterpillar	Eric Carle	Eric Carle	Philomel Books	1969
Of Lucky Pebbles and Mermaid's Tears	Mimi Gregoire Carpenter	Mimi Gregoire Carpenter	Beachcomber (Studio) Press	1994
The Great Kapok Tree	Lynne Cherry	Lynne Cherry	Trumpet	1990
Jack-in-the-Box	Joy Cowley	Philip Webb	Shortland Publications	1981
The Screaming Mean Machine	Joy Cowley	David Cox	Scholastic, Inc.	1993
Parade	Donald Crews	Donald Crews	Mulberry Books	1983
School Bus	Donald Crews	Donald Crews	Greenwillow Books	1984
Look...a Butterfly	David Cutts	Eulala Conner	Troll Associates	1982
Why the Sun and Moon Live in the Sky	Elphinstone Dayrell	Blair Lent	Scholastic, Inc.	1968
Bear Party	William Pene Du Bois	William Pene Du Bois	Puffin Books	1987
Eating the Alphabet	Lois Ehlert	Lois Ehlert	Trumpet Club	1989
Fish Eyes	Lois Ehlert	Lois Ehlert	Trumpet Club	1990
Hattie and the Fox	Mem Fox	Patricia Mullins	D. C. Heath and Company	1986

(continued)

Title	Author	Illustrator	Publisher	Copyright
Millions of Cats	Wanda Ga'g	Wanda Ga'g	Scholastic, Inc.	1928
Ten Little Rabbits	Virginia Grossman	Sylvia Long	Trumpet Club	1991
Fall Leaves Fall	Zoe Hall	Shari Halpren	Scholastic, Inc.	2000
Chameleons Are Cool	Martin Jenkins	Sue Shields	Scholastic, Inc.	1997
The Quilt Story	Tony Johnston	Tomie de Paola	G. P. Putnam's Sons	1985
Round Trip	Ann Jonas	Ann Jonas	Greenwillow Books	1983
Jennie's Hat	Ezra Jack Keats	Ezra Jack Keats	Harper & Row	1996
101 Dalmatians	Walt Disney's classic adapted by Justine Korman	Bill Langley and Ron Dias	Western Publishing Company	1991
Alexander and the Wind-Up Mouse	Leo Lionni	Leo Lionni	Scholastic, Inc.	1969
the alphabet tree	Leo Lionni	Leo Lionni	Trumpet Club	1968
The Biggest House in the World	Leo Lionni	Leo Lionni	Alfred A. Knopf, Inc.	1968
Swimmy	Leo Lionni	Leo Lionni	Alfred A. Knopf, Inc.	1963
Alison's Zinnia	Anita Lobel	Anita Lobel	Greenwillow Books	1990
Brown Bear, Brown Bear, What Do You See?	Bill Martin, Jr.	Eric Carle	Holt, Rinehart and Winston	1983
Up and Down on the Merry-Go-Round	Bill Martin, Jr., and John Archambault	Ted Rand	Henry Holt and Company	1985
Papagayo	Gerald McDermott	Gerald McDermott	Harcourt Brace Jovanovich	1992
Raven	Gerald McDermott	Gerald McDermott	Scholastic, Inc.	1993
Elmer	David McKee	David McKee	Lorthrop, Lee, & Shepard	1968
The Mountain That Loved a Bird	Alice McLerran	Eric Carle	Scholastic, Inc.	1985
Purple, Green and Yellow	Robert Munsch	Helene Desputeaux	Annick Press Ltd.	1992
The Ant and the Elephant	Bill Peet	Bill Peet	Houghton Mifflin	1972
The Night Sky	Alice Pernick	Lisa Desimini	Scholastic, Inc.	1994
The Gingerbread Man		Bonnie and Bill Rutherford	Merrigold	1963
Where the Wild Things Are	Maurice Sendak	Maurice Sendak	HarperCollins	1988
The Monster at the End of This Book	Jon Stone	Mike Smollin	Western Publishing Co.	1971
The Popcorn Dragon	Jane Thayer	Lisa McCue	Scholastic, Inc.	1953
A Tree Is Nice	Janice May Udry	Marc Simont	Harper Trophy	1987
Owl Babies	Martin Waddell	Patrick Benson	Candlewick Press	1992
No Dodos	Amanda Wallwork	Amanda Wallwork	Scholastic, Inc.	1993
Apple Bird	Brian Wildsmith	Brian Wildsmith	Oxford University Press	1983
Circus	Brian Wildsmith	Brian Wildsmith	Oxford University Press	1970

abstract art—A visual interpretation with little regard to realistic representation.

aesthetic—Appreciation of the beauty in art or nature.

art appreciation—Awareness of the aesthetic values in artwork.

art medium—Materials used to create an artwork.

art museum—A building where artwork is displayed.

art reproduction—Photographic duplication of an original piece of art.

asymmetrical—Artwork that looks balanced when the parts are arranged differently on each side.

background—The part in an artwork that looks farther away or is behind other parts.

balance—The arrangement of visual elements so that the parts seem to be equally important.

basic shapes—Circle, square, triangle, rectangle.

brayer—A roller used to apply paint or ink.

cityscape—A view or picture of a city.

collage—Artwork made by assembling and gluing materials to a flat surface.

composition—The arrangement of design elements into proper relation.

concept—A general idea or understanding.

construct—To create an artwork by putting materials together.

contour—The outline of a shape or form.

contrast—Great difference between two things.

cool colors—Colors that remind people of cool things. They often create a calm or sad feeling. Blue, green, and purple are cool colors.

crayon etching—Scratching through one layer of crayon to let another layer of crayon show through.

crayon resist—When painting over crayons with water-based paints, the paint will not cover the crayons because crayons are either wax or oil based and it resists the water.

creative—Having the ability to make things in a new or different way.

cubism—A style of art where shapes or forms seem to be divided or have many edges.

design—The ordered arrangement of art elements in an artwork.

design elements—The basic visual tools an artist works with: line, shape, form, color, value, and texture.

design principles—The way an artist uses the design elements: unity, balance, rhythm, movement, variety, and repetition.

detail—Small items or parts.

drawing—Describing something by means of line.

emphasis—Special stress of one or more art design components.

expressionism—A style of art where a definite mood or feeling is depicted.

Fantasy Art—Artwork that is meant to look unreal, strange, or dreamlike.

foreground—The part in an artwork that seems near or close.

form—A three-dimensional design.

free form—A free-flowing, imaginative shape.

geometric shapes—Shapes that have smooth edges.

horizontal—A line that goes from side to side.

illusion—A misleading image.

imagination—Creative ability.

intermediate colors—Colors that are made by mixing a primary color and a secondary color. Red orange, red violet, blue green, blue violet, yellow orange, yellow green are intermediate colors.

landscape—Artwork that depicts an outdoor scene.

line—A mark made by a moving point.

mixed media—Artwork made up of different materials or techniques.

mobile—A sculpture with parts that move by air currents.

model—A person who poses for an artist.

montage—A composite picture made by combining several separate pictures.

mosaic—Artwork made with small pieces.

movement—The rhythmic qualities of a design.

mural—A large artwork created or displayed on a wall.

negative space—Empty space in a design.

neutral colors—Brown, black, white, and gray.

non objective—A style of art where the main ideas or feelings come from the design created with colors, lines, and shapes. It does not show objects or scenes.

opaque—Not transparent.

original—Artwork that looks very different from other artwork.

overlap—One part that covers some of another part.

pattern—Lines, colors, or shapes repeated over and over in a planned way. A model or guide for making something.

perspective—The extent to which the shapes of objects and distances between them look familiar or correct.

pop art—A style of art that uses everyday objects as the subject.

portrait—Artwork that shows the face of a person.

positive space—The actual shapes or figures in a design.

pose—A special position of the body.

primary colors—Colors from which other colors can be made. Red, blue, and yellow are primary colors.

print—To press and lift something with ink or paint on it.

profile—The side view of something.

proportion—The size, location, or amount of something as compared to something else.

radial—Lines or shapes that come out from the center point.

realism—A style of artwork that shows objects or scenes as they look in everyday life.

relief—Something that stands out from a flat background.

repetition—The repeated use of the same design elements.

renaissance—A time in European history (A.D. 1400–1600) after the Middle Ages. Artists during this time discovered many new ways to create things.

rhythm—A repetition of design elements to create a visual balance.

romantic—A style of artwork in which the main ideas are to show adventures, imaginary events, faraway places, or strong feelings.

secondary colors—Colors that can be mixed from two primary colors. Orange, green, and purple are secondary colors.

shade—The darkness of colors. A color mixed with black.

shape—The outline edge or flat surface of a form.

space—An empty place or area.

stencil—A flat material with a cutout design.

still life—An artwork that consists of nonliving objects.

style—An artist's personal way of creating art.

symmetry—Parts arranged the same way on both sides.

technique—A special way to create artwork.

texture—The way something feels or the way it looks like it feels.

three-dimensional—Artwork that can be measured three ways: height, width, and depth.

tint—A light color. A color mixed with white.

transparent—Transmitting light.

two-dimensional—Artwork that is flat and measured in two ways: height and width.

unity—The quality of having all parts look like they belong.

value—The lightness or darkness of a color.

variety—Having differences.

vertical—A line that runs up and down.

warm colors—Colors that remind people of warm things. Red, yellow, and orange are warm colors.

References

Art and activities. San Diego: Publishers' Development Corp.

Barton, J. (1999). Using multicultural children's literature to teach science. *The NERA Journal, 35*(2) 7–10.

Blake, M. E., & Bartel, V. (1999). Storytelling in the classroom: Personal narratives and pre-service teachers. *The NERA Journal, 35*(2) 3–6.

Chapman, L. (1985). Discover art. Worcester, MA: Davis Publications.

Ernst, K. (1994). *Picturing learning: Artists and writers in the classroom.* Portsmouth, NH: Heinemann.

Horn, G. F., & Smith, G. S. (1971). *Experiencing art in the elementary school.* Dallas: Hendrick-Long Publishing Company.

Howard, P., & Wilson, M. (1994). Primary explorations: A team approach. *The picturebook: Source and resource for art education.* Reston, VA: National Art Education Association.

Lansing, K. M., & Richards, A. E. (1981). *The elementary teacher's art handbook.* New York: Holt, Rinehart and Winston.

Lanthier, H., & Rich, B. (1999). Connecting art education and children's books. *The NERA Journal, 35*(2) 24–29.

Libby, W. M. L. (2000). *Using art to make art.* Clifton Park, NY: Delmar Learning.

Libby, W. M. L. (2001). *Enriching the curriculum with art experiences.* Clifton Park, NY: Delmar Learning.

Marantz, K. (1994). Art of the picturebook: The road from Caldecott to Sendak. *The picturebook: Source and resource for art education.* Reston, VA: National Art Education Association.

School arts. Worcester, MA: Davis Publication.

Wachowiak, F., & Ramsay, T. (1971). *Emphasis: Art.* Scranton: Intext Educational Publishers.